Practice Papers for SQA Exams

Intermediate 2

Chemistry

Introduction	3
Topic Index	6
Exam 1	9
Exam 2	27
Exam 3	49
Worked Answers	69

Text © 2010 Barry McBride
Design and layout © 2010 Leckie & Leckie

01/100510

All rights reserved. No part of this publication may be reproduced, stored in a retrieval system, or transmitted in any form or by any means, electronic, mechanical, photocopying, recording or otherwise, without prior permission in writing from Leckie & Leckie Ltd. Legal action will be taken by Leckie & Leckie Ltd against any infringement of our copyright.

The right of Barry McBride to be identified as the Author of this Work has been asserted by him in accordance with sections 77 and 78 of the Copyright, Designs and Patents Act 1988.

ISBN 978-1-84372-801-6

Published by
Leckie & Leckie
An imprint of HarperCollins*Publishers*
Westerhill Road, Bishopbriggs, Glasgow, G64 2QT
T: 0870 460 7662 F: 0870 787 1720
E-mail: enquiries@leckieandleckie.co.uk
Web: www.leckieandleckie.co.uk

A CIP Catalogue record for this book is available from the British Library.

Questions and answers in this book do not emanate from SQA. All of our entirely new and original Practice Papers have been written by experienced authors working directly for the publisher.

Introduction

Layout of the book

This book contains practice exam papers, which mirror the actual SQA exam as much as possible. The layout, paper colour and question level are all similar to the actual exam that you will sit, so that you are familiar with what the exam paper will look like.

The answer section is at the back of the book. Each question has a worked answer or solution so that you can see how the right answer has been arrived at. The answers also include practical tips on how to tackle certain types of questions, details of how marks are awarded and advice on just what the examiners will be looking for.

Revision advice is provided in this introductory section of the book, so please read on!

How to use this book

The Practice Papers can be used in two main ways:

1. You can complete an entire practice paper as preparation for the final exam. If you would like to use the book in this way, you can complete the practice paper under exam style conditions by setting yourself a time for each paper and answering it as well as possible without using any references or notes. Alternatively, you can answer the practice paper questions as a revision exercise, using your notes to produce a model answer. Your teacher may mark these for you.

2. You can use the Topic Index at the front of this book to find all the questions within the book that deal with a specific topic. This allows you to focus specifically on areas that you particularly want to revise or, if you are midway through your course, it lets you practise answering exam-style questions for just those topics that you have studied.

Revision advice

Work out a revision timetable for each week's work in advance – remember to cover all of your subjects and to leave time for homework and breaks. For example:

Day	6pm–6.45pm	7pm–8pm	8.15pm–9pm	9.15pm–10pm
Monday	Homework	Homework	English revision	Chemistry revision
Tuesday	Maths revision	Physics revision	Homework	Free
Wednesday	Geography revision	Modern studies revision	English revision	French revision
Thursday	Homework	Maths revision	Chemistry revision	Free
Friday	Geography revision	French revision	Free	Free
Saturday	Free	Free	Free	Free
Sunday	Modern studies revision	Maths revision	Chemistry revision	Homework

Make sure that you have at least one evening free a week to relax, socialise and re-charge your batteries. It also gives your brain a chance to process the information that you have been feeding it all week.

Arrange your study time into sessions, with a break between sessions of between 30 minutes and 1 hour, e.g. 6pm–6.45pm, 7pm–8pm, 8.15pm–9pm. Try to start studying as early as possible in the evening when your brain is still alert and be aware that the longer you put off starting, the harder it will be to start!

Study a different subject in each session, except for the day before an exam.

Do something different during your breaks between study sessions – have a cup of tea, or listen to some music. Don't let your 15 minutes expand into 20 or 25 minutes though!

Have your class notes and any textbooks available for your revision to hand as well as plenty of blank paper, a pen, etc. You may like to make keyword sheets like the geography example below:

Keyword	Meaning
Anticyclone	An area of high pressure
Secondary Industry	Industries which manufacture things
Erosion	The process of wearing down the landscape

Finally, forget or ignore all or some of the advice in this section if you are happy with your present way of studying. Everyone revises differently, so find a way that works for you!

Transfer your knowledge

These practice papers will also be a useful revision tool in addition to your class notes and text books as they will help you to get used to answering exam style questions. You may find as you work through the questions that they refer to a case-study or an example that you haven't come across before. Don't worry! You should be able to transfer your knowledge of a topic or theme to a new example. The enhanced answer section at the back will demonstrate how to read and interpret the question to identify the topic being examined and how to apply your course knowledge in order to answer the question successfully.

Command words

In the practice papers and in the exam itself, a number of command words will be used in the questions. These command words are used to show you how you should answer the question – some words indicate that you should write more than others. If you familiarise yourself with these command words, it will help you to structure your answers more effectively.

Command Word	Meaning/Explanation
Name, state, identify, list	Giving a list is acceptable here – as a general rule you will get one mark for each point you give.
Suggest	Give more than a list – perhaps a proposal or an idea.
Outline	Give a brief description or overview of what you are talking about.
Describe	Give more detail than you would in an outline, and use examples where you can.
Explain	Discuss why an action has been taken or an outcome reached – what are the reasons and/or processes behind it?
Justify	Give reasons for your answer, stating why you have taken an action or reached a particular conclusion.
Define	Give the meaning of the term.
Compare	Give the key features of 2 different items or ideas and discuss their similarities and/or their differences.

In the Exam

Watch your time and pace yourself carefully. Work out roughly how much time you can spend on each answer and try to stick to this.

Be clear before the exam what the instructions are likely to be, e.g. how many questions you should answer in each section. The practice papers will help you to become familiar with the exam's instructions.

Read the question thoroughly before you begin to answer it – make sure you know exactly what the question is asking you to do. If the question is in sections, e.g. 15a, 15b, 15c, etc, make sure that you can answer each section before you start writing.

Plan your answer by jotting down keywords, a mind map or reminders of the important things to include in your answer. Cross them off as you deal with them and check them before you move on to the next question to make sure that you haven't forgotten anything.

Don't repeat yourself as you will not get any more marks for saying the same thing twice. This also applies to annotated diagrams, which will not get you any extra marks if the information is repeated in the written part of your answer.

Give proper explanations. A common error is to give descriptions rather than explanations. If you are asked to explain something, you should be giving reasons. Check your answer to an 'explain' question and make sure that you have used plenty of linking words and phrases such as 'because', 'this means that', 'therefore', 'so', 'so that', 'due to', 'since' and 'the reason is'.

Use the resources provided. Some questions will ask you to 'describe and explain' and provide an example or a case-study for you to work from. Make sure that you take any relevant data from these resources.

Good luck!

Topic Index

Topic	Exam 1	Exam 2	Exam 3	Knowledge for Prelim			Knowledge for SQA Exam		
				Have difficulty	Still needs work	OK	Have difficulty	Still needs work	OK
Unit 1 – Energy Matters									
Substances	A: 1	A: 1, 2 B: 2b	A: 1, 2, 4, 7						
Reaction Rates	A: 3, 4 B: 3b	A: 3, 4 B: 5a, 5b, 5c	A: 3, 5 B: 14d						
The Structure of the Atom	A: 5, 6 B: 2a, 2b, 2c	A: 5 B: 1a, 1b, 1c	A: 6						
Bonding, Structure and properties.	A: 7, 9, 12 B: 1a, 1b, 1c, 12	A: 6, 7, 8, 9 B: 6a, 6b, 6c	A: 8, 9 B: 3c, 12a, 12c						
Chemical Formulas and Balancing Equations	A: 2, 8, 23 B: 3c, 8b	B: 2a	A: 10 B: 12b						
The Mole	B: 8b, 14	B: 3c, 12	B: 6c						
PPA 1 – Reaction Rate (Concentration)	B: 7a, 7b, 7c		B: 2a, 2b, 2c, 2d						
PPA 2 – Reaction Rate (Temperature)									
PPA 3 – Electrolysis		B: 9a, 9b, 9c							

Topic	Exam 1	Exam 2	Exam 3	Knowledge for Prelim			Knowledge for SQA Exam		
				Have difficulty	Still needs work	OK	Have difficulty	Still needs work	OK
Unit 2 – Carbon Compounds									
Fuels	A: 10, 11 B: 4c	A: 12, 13	A: 12, 17 B: 10c, 14a, 14b, 14c						
Hydrocarbons	A: 14, 15 B: 4a. 10b, 11a, 11b, 11c, 11d, 11e	A: 14, 15 B: 13a, 13b, 13c, 13d, 13e	A: 13, 14 B: 6a, 6b, 8c						
Reactions of Carbon Compounds	A: 13, 16, 18, 19	A: 17 B: 8a, 8b, 8c	A: 11, 15, 16						
Plastics and Synthetic Fibres	A: 17 B: 10a, 10c	B: 14a, 14b	A: 20 B: 13a, 13b, 13c						
Natural Products	A: 13, 20	A: 18, 19, 20	A: 18, 19 B: 1a, 1b, 1c, 1d						
PPA 1 – Testing for Unsaturation		B: 7a, 7b, 7c, 7d							
PPA 2 – Cracking	B: 6a, 6b, 6c, 6d								
PPA 3 – Hydrolysis of Starch			B: 5a, 5b, 5c						

Topic	Exam 1	Exam 2	Exam 3	Knowledge for Prelim			Knowledge for SQA Exam		
				Have difficulty	Still needs work	OK	Have difficulty	Still needs work	OK
Unit 3 – Acids, Bases and Metals									
Acids and Bases	A: 21, 22, 9c, 9d	A: 22, 23, 24	A: 25, 26 B: 4a, 4b						
Salt Preparation	A: 24, 25, 26 B: 8a	A: 21, 25 B: 4a	A: 29, 30 B: 9						
Metals	A: 27, 28, 29, 30 B: 13a, 13b, 13c, 13d	A: 10, 26, 27, 30 B: 3a, 4b, 10a, 10b, 10c, 10d	A: 21, 22, 23, 24, 28 B: 11a, 11b, 11c, 12d						
PPA 1 – Preparation of a Salt	B: 5a, 5b, 5c, 5d								
PPA 2 – Factors affecting Voltage			B: 7a, 7b, 7c						
PPA 3 – Reaction of Metals with Oxygen		B: 11a, 11b, 11c							
Problem Solving	B: 3a, 4b, 9a, 9b	A: 11, 14, 28, 29 B: 2c, 2d, 3b, 4c	A: 15, 27 B: 3a, 3b, 8a, 8b, 10a, 10b						

Exam 1

Answer sheet for Section A:

Intermediate 2 Chemistry
Practice Papers for SQA Exams

Please select your answer using a single mark e.g. A ☐ B ▄ C ☐ D ☐

Intermediate 2 Chemistry

| Practice Papers for SQA Exams | Time allowed: 2 hours | Exam 1 |

Fill in these boxes and read what is printed below.

Full name of school

Town

Forename(s)

Surname

Read each question carefully.

Attempt **all** questions.

Write your answers on the blank paper provided.

Write as neatly as possible.

Answer in sentences wherever possible.

Read closely

1. For Section A, you should use an HB pencil and, where neccesary, a rubber.
2. Each answer is **either** A, B, C or D. When you have decided your answer, use your pencil to put a line in the appropriate space on the answer sheet. (See the example below.)
3. Each question has **only one correct** answer.
4. Do not do any rough working on the answer sheet: use a separate sheet of paper.

Sample question

The surface area:volume ratio of a cube with edges 1 cm is

A 1:1

B 3:1

C 6:1

D 12:1

The correct answer is **C** – 6:1. This answer has been clearly marked in **pencil** below.

Changing an answer

If you need to change an answer, carefully rub out your original, then use your pencil to fill in the answer you now want. Below, the answer has been changed to **D**.

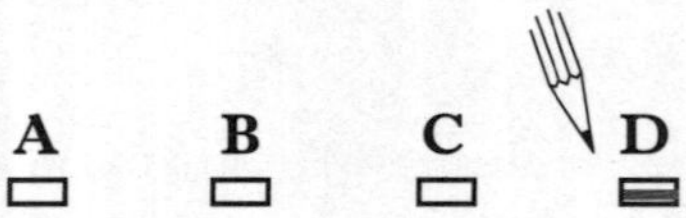

SECTION A

1. Which of the following elements was discovered before 1775?

    A Bromine

    B Oxygen

    C Magnesium

    D Silicon

2. When solid lithium hydroxide is dissolved in water, a solution containing both hydroxide ions and lithium ions is formed. Which equation correctly shows this change?

    A $LiOH(s) + H_2O(aq) \rightarrow Li^+(aq) + OH^-(aq)$

    B $LiOH(s) + H_2O(l) \rightarrow Li^+(aq) + OH^-(aq)$

    C $LiOH(l) + H_2O(l) \rightarrow Li^+(aq) + OH^-(aq)$

    D $LiOH(s) + H_2O(aq) \rightarrow Li^+(l) + OH^-(aq)$

3. The graph below shows the change in the concentration of a reactant with time as the reaction proceeds.

    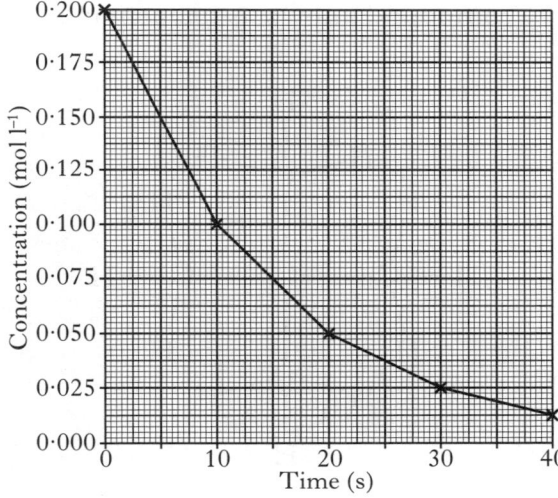

    What is the average rate of this reaction, in $mol\ l^{-1} s^{-1}$, for the first 20 seconds?

    A 0.01

    B 0.0025

    C 0.005

    D 0.0075

4. Scientists investigating the effects of acid rain on limestone experimented with different concentrations of acids, on different sized pieces of limestone, at different temperatures.

    Which of the following conditions would result in the slowest rate of the reaction?

    A Low temperature, small particle size and high concentration

    B High temperature, small particle size and high concentration

    C High temperature, large particle size and low concentration

    D Low temperature, large particle size and low concentration

5. Isotopes of an element have different

    A atomic numbers

    B mass numbers

    C number of electrons

    D number of protons

6. An element has an atomic number of 13 and a mass number of 27. The number of electrons in its atoms is

    A 13

    B 14

    C 27

    D 40

7. Which substance exists as diatomic molecules?

    A Carbon tetrachloride

    B Sulphur dioxide

    C Sodium fluoride

    D Nitrogen monoxide

8. What is the charge on a titanium ion in $TiCl_3$?

   A 1+
   B 1−
   C 3+
   D 3−

9. Metallic bonds are due to

   A an attraction between positive ions and delocalised electrons
   B a shared pair of electrons
   C an attraction between positive ions and negative ions
   D an attraction between negative ions and delocalised electrons

10. Crude oil can be separated by the process of fractional distillation because the hydrocarbons it contains all have different

    A viscosities
    B flammabilities
    C boiling points
    D solubilities

11. Which of the following molecules is most likely to be found in petrol?

    A CH_4
    B C_2H_6
    C C_8H_{18}
    D C_9H_{20}

12. Which of the following substances does **not** have a covalent network structure?

    A Diamond
    B Sulphur
    C Silicon dioxide
    D Silicon carbide

13. Margarines are hardened fats produced from vegetable oils. The melting point of the oil is increased by

    A adding hydrogen
    B adding water
    C removing hydrogen
    D removing water

14. Shown below is the structure of a compound known as neopentane.

    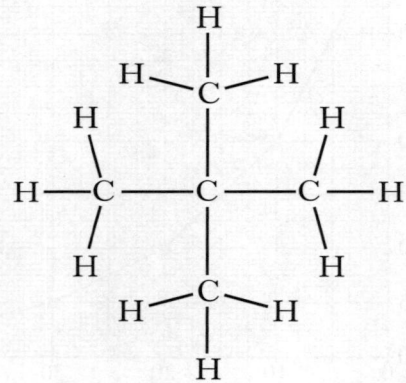

    The systematic name of the above compound is

    A 3,2-dimethylbutane
    B 2,2-dimethylpropane
    C 2,3-dimethylbutane
    D 3,2-dimethylpropane

15. The first three members of the alkynes homologous series are:

H—C≡C—H

H—C≡C—CH₃ (with H's shown)

H—C≡C—CH₂—CH₃ (with H's shown)

The general formula of this homologous series is

A C_nH_{2n}

B C_nH_{2n-2}

C C_nH_{2n+2}

D C_nH_n

16. Ethanol can be produced from ethene by

A hydration

B condensation

C hydrolysis

D dehydration

17. Which of the following is made from an unsaturated monomer?

A Polyamide

B Polyester

C Nylon

D Polyethene

18. Which of the following molecules is **not** an isomer of but-1-ene?

A But-2-ene

B 2-methylprop-1-ene

C Cyclobutane

D 2-methylpropane

19. The diagram shown represents

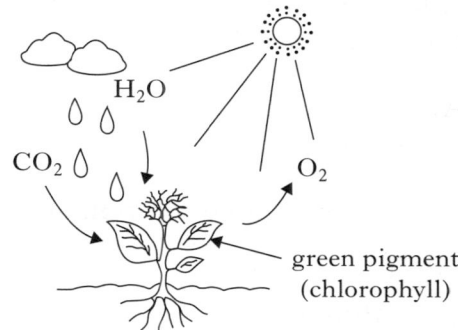

A combustion

B fermentation

C photosynthesis

D respiration

20. A solution containing two carbohydrates was tested separately with iodine and Benedict's solution. The iodine turned blue/black and the Benedict's solution turned brick red on heating with the solution. The two carbohydrates contained in the solution could have been

A glucose and fructose

B starch and sucrose

C starch and glucose

D fructose and sucrose

21. 0·25 mol of ascorbic acid was dissolved in 500 cm³ of water. What was the concentration of the solution formed?

A 0·25 mol l⁻¹

B 0·50 mol l⁻¹

C 0·75 mol l⁻¹

D 1·00 mol l⁻¹

22. A 0·01 mol l⁻¹ solution of nitric acid can be described as

A a concentrated solution of a strong acid

B a concentrated solution of a weak acid

C a dilute solution of a strong acid

D a dilute solution of a weak acid.

23. $Cu^{2+}(aq) + e^- \rightarrow Cu^+(aq)$

This ion electron equation represents

A reduction of copper(II) ions

B reduction of copper(I) ions

C oxidation of copper(II) ions

D oxidation of copper(I) ions.

24. Which of the following compounds is classed as a salt?

A Sodium oxide

B Calcium chloride

C Sulphur dioxide

D Hydrogen chloride

25. Which of the following can be produced by a precipitation reaction?

A Sodium chloride

B Lithium chloride

C Copper chloride

D Silver chloride

26. Which of the following gases would react with an alkaline solution?

A Nitrogen

B Sulphur dioxide

C Ammonia

D Neon

27. Which pair of metals will produce an electron flow in the direction shown?

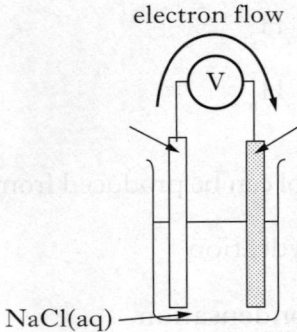

A Mg/Zn

B Zn/Mg

C Cu/Zn

D Ag/Zn

28. The corrosion of iron can be slowed by

A connecting the iron to the negative terminal of a battery

B sitting the iron in salty water

C connecting the iron to the positive terminal of a battery

D wrapping a piece of copper wire round the iron.

29. Which of these metals can displace iron from a solution of iron(II) sulphate but **not** displace magnesium from a solution of magnesium sulphate?

A Zinc

B Copper

C Calcium

D Tin

30. Which of the following metals is obtained from its ore by electrolysis?

A Mercury

B Gold

C Aluminium

D Iron

SECTION B

1. In a molecule of methane the atoms are held together by sharing electrons to form bonds. The bonds formed are known as covalent bonds.

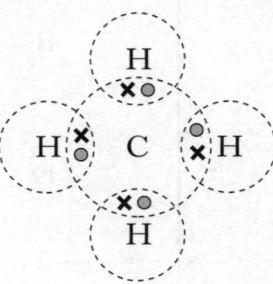

   (a) Explain fully how a covalent bond holds atoms together.

   _____

   _____

   _____   1

   (b) Draw a diagram to show the shape of a methane molecule.

   1

   (c) What is meant by the term molecule?

   _____

   _____   1

2. The nuclide notation shows the atomic number and mass number of an isotope. The nuclide notation for an isotope of helium is $^{2}_{2}$He.

   (a) An isotope of sodium has atomic number 11 and mass number 23. What is the nuclide notation for this isotope of sodium?

   _____   1

   (b) How many neutrons does this isotope of sodium contain?

   _____   1

   (c) There are 13 isotopes of sodium, all of which are electrically neutral. What does this suggest about the proton to electron ratio in all the isotopes of sodium?

   _____   1

3. Nitrogen dioxide can be produced in a number of ways but industrially it is produced using the Ostwald process. In the first stage of this process, ammonia and air are passed over a hot catalyst to produce nitrogen monoxide.

   (a) What **type** of element is used as the catalyst in this process?

   _____ 1

   (b) The catalyst used is a heterogeneous catalyst. What is a heterogeneous catalyst?

   _____ 1

   (c) In the second stage of this process the nitrogen monoxide combines with oxygen in an exothermic reaction to produce nitrogen dioxide. Balance the equation for this reaction.

   $$NO(g) + O_2(g) \rightleftharpoons NO_2(g)$$

   _____ 1

4. Volatile organic compounds (VOCs) are organic compounds that can cause damage to the Earth's atmosphere. They may also be harmful or toxic. They are used as solvents in paints: the VOC content is displayed on most paint cans.

   (a) An example of a VOC compound used in paints is methanal which is the first member of the aldehyde homologous series. Methanal has the structural formula

   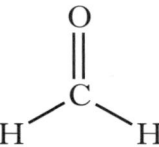

   What is a homologous series?

   _____
   _____
   _____ 1

   (b) What is the molecular formula of methanal?

   _____ 1

   (c) Methanal is very flammable. What are the two products of complete combustion of methanal?

   _____ 1

5. In a PPA, crystals of magnesium sulphate can be prepared by reacting magnesium carbonate with sulphuric acid.

(a) Write the chemical equation for this reaction. (There is no need to balance the equation.)

(b) The three steps involved in preparing magnesium sulphate are shown below.

1. 'Reaction' step   2. 'Filtration' step   3. 'Evaporation' step

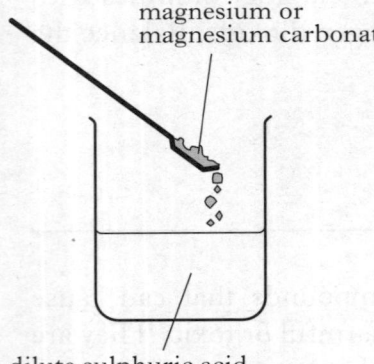
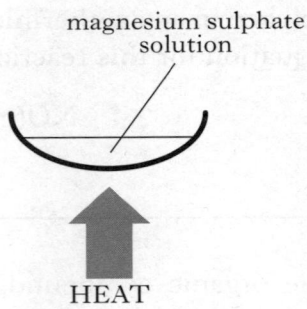

Draw the labelled diagram for the filtration step.

(c) In the 'Reaction' step, how can you tell that the reaction is complete?

(d) Why must the magnesium carbonate be added in excess to the sulphuric acid?

DO NOT WRITE IN THIS MARGIN

MARKS

6. Catalytic cracking is a process in which large hydrocarbon molecules, produced from fractional distillation of crude oil, are broken down into smaller, more profitable molecules.

(*a*) The catalytic cracking of paraffin is performed in the lab as part of the PPA, 'Cracking'. Label the diagram of the apparatus used to crack liquid paraffin.

1

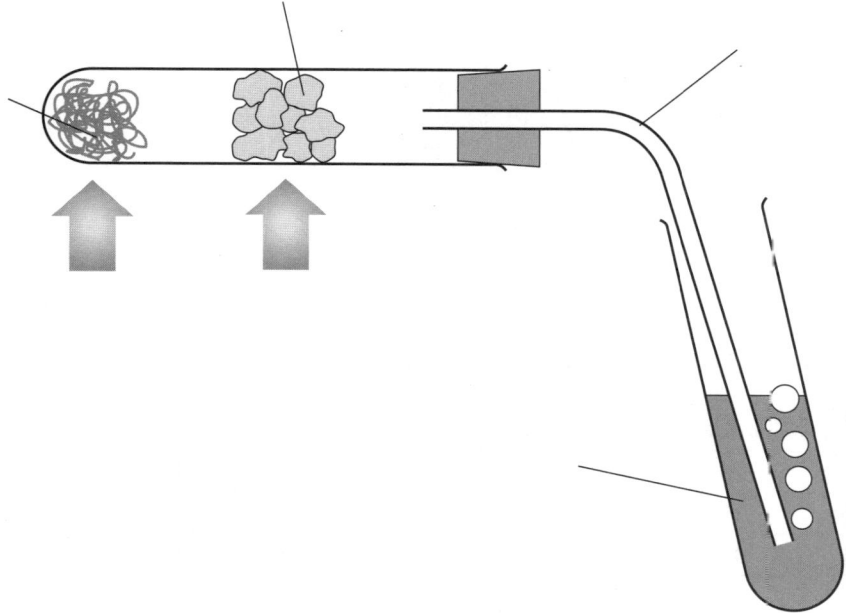

(*b*) One of the dangers associated with this experiment is 'suck back'. Describe how this danger can be avoided.

____

________________________________ **1**

(*c*) The equation for one catalytic cracking process is shown below. Complete the equation.

$$C_{12}H_{26} \rightarrow C_8H_{18} + ______$$ **1**

(*d*) One of the products of catalytic cracking is always unsaturated. Why is it not possible to produce only saturated products?

____

________________________________ **1**

7. The reaction between sodium thiosulphate and dilute hydrochloric acid is used in a PPA to investigate the effect that temperature has on the rate of reaction. During the reaction, solid sulphur appears in the solution.

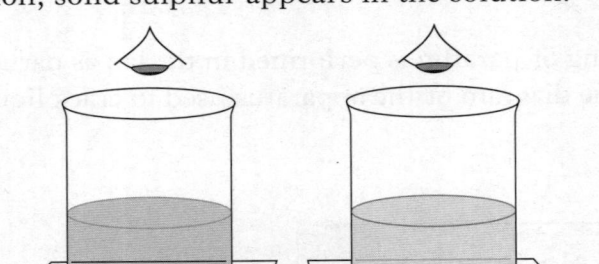

(a) How was the end-point of the reaction determined?

(b) The results obtained were recorded in the table below

Temperature (°C)	Reaction time (s)	Rate (s^{-1})
20	70	0·0143
29	40	0·0250
38	25	0·0400
49	12	

Complete the table to show the rate of reaction at 49°C.

(c) What conclusion can be drawn from these results?

8. Together with other iron compounds, iron(II) sulphate can be used to treat iron-deficiency anaemia. Iron(II) sulphate can be produced by reacting iron(II) oxide with sulphuric acid.

$$FeO(s) + H_2SO_4(aq) \rightarrow FeSO_4(aq) + H_2O(l)$$

(a) Name the type of reaction that is taking place.

(b) A pharmaceutical company reacts 50 g of iron(II) oxide with excess sulphuric acid. What mass of iron(II) sulphate can be made from this mass of iron(II) oxide?

9. The Haber process produces ammonia (NH$_3$) by combining nitrogen and hydrogen. The nitrogen required comes from the air and the hydrogen from methane. They are converted into ammonia by passing them over an iron catalyst at a moderately high temperature of 500°C using high pressure. Not all of the nitrogen and hydrogen is converted into ammonia. The unreacted nitrogen and hydrogen are put back into the reaction chamber to make the whole process more economic. Nothing is wasted.

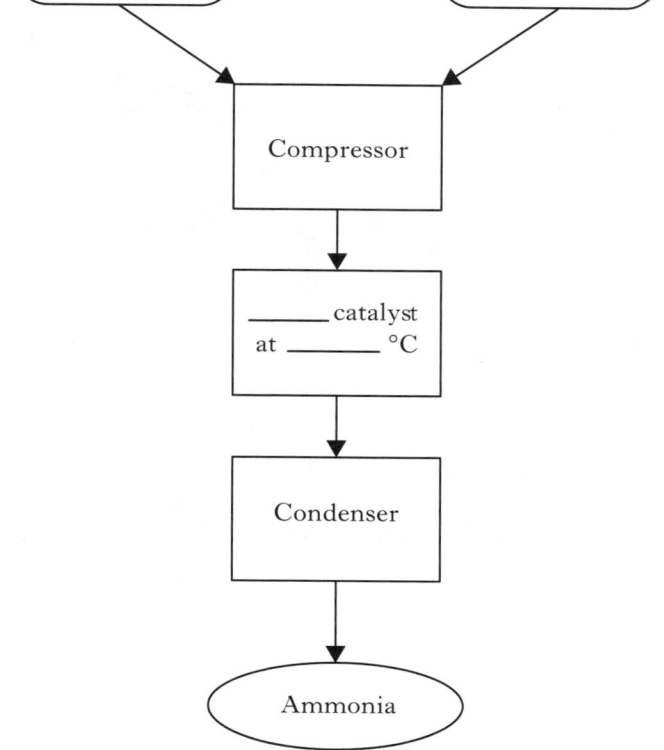

(a) Use the information above to complete the flow diagram for the Haber process.

(b) Add a line to the flow diagram to show the unreacted hydrogen and nitrogen being recycled.

(c) Ammonia is classed as a weak alkali. Why is meant by the term weak alkali?

(d) Sodium hydroxide is described as a strong alkali. Write a formula equation to show its dissociation in water.

DO NOT WRITE IN THIS MARGIN

MARKS

10. Kevlar was a polymer that was developed in 1965 and was first used in the tyres of racing cars to give them strength. It is also used as body armour.

(*a*) Apart from its strength, suggest another property of Kevlar that makes it suitable for use as body armour.

____ **1**

(*b*) Shown below are the structures of the monomers that are combined to form Kevlar. What name is given to the highlighted functional group?

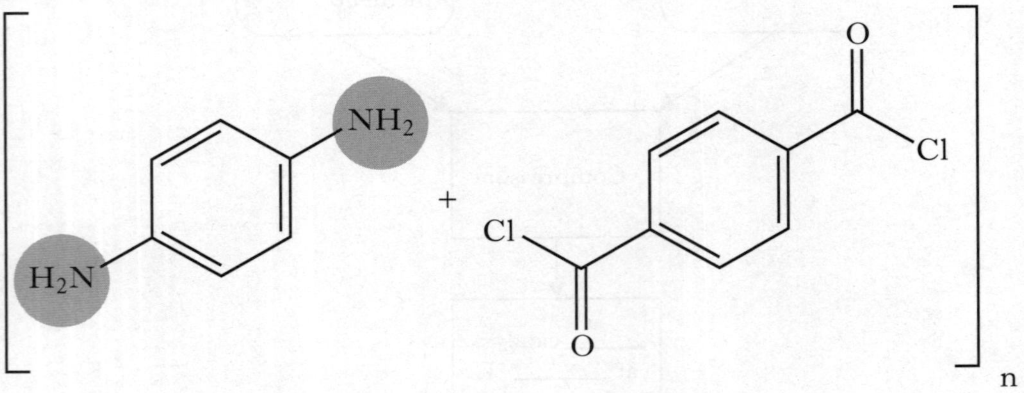

____ **1**

(*c*) What type of polymerisation reaction forms Kevlar?

____ **1**

DO NOT WRITE IN THIS MARGIN

MARKS

11. Formic acid (methanoic acid) is contained in the stings of many insects such as wood ants and is also present in stinging nettles

(*a*) Draw the full structural formula of formic acid. **1**

(*b*) Ethyl methanoate is produced from methanoic acid and an alcohol. Name the alcohol.

____ **1**

(*c*) Describe an experiment you could carry out to make a sample of this ester in the laboratory. Include a labelled diagram of the apparatus and the names of any chemicals used.

____

____

____ **3**

(*d*) Apart from wearing safety goggles, suggest any safety precautions that must be considered whilst carrying out this experiment.

____ **1**

(*e*) Draw the full structural formula of ethyl methanoate. **1**

12. The physical properties of a substance are due to the bonds that are present in the substance. Complete the table below.

Name of substance	Bonding	Conductor or non-conductor	State at room temperature
Sodium chloride		Non-conductor	
Sodium	Metallic		
Chlorine	Covalent		
Carbon (graphite)			Solid

13. When copper is added to a solution of silver nitrate, the solution turns blue and the copper appears to turn from brown to silver.

$$2AgNO_3(aq) + Cu(s) \rightarrow Cu(NO_3)_2(aq) + 2Ag(s)$$

(a) Name the type of reaction that is taking place.

_____

(b) Name the spectator ion in this reaction.

_____

(c) What does this reaction suggest about the reactivity of silver in comparison to copper?

_____

(d) Write the ion-electron equation for the oxidation step in this reaction.

14. Mrs Glancy is making a solution of sodium hydroxide for her chemistry class. She requires 250 cm³ of 2 mol l⁻¹ sodium hydroxide solution to perform a neutralisation reaction with hydrochloric acid. What mass of sodium hydroxide is required to produce this solution?

Exam 2

Answer sheet for Section A:

Intermediate 2 Chemistry
Practice Papers for SQA Exams

Please select your answer using a single mark e.g. A B C D
                                                   ☐ ▬ ☐ ☐

	A	B	C	D		A	B	C	D
1.	☐	☐	☐	☐	16.	☐	☐	☐	☐
2.	☐	☐	☐	☐	17.	☐	☐	☐	☐
3.	☐	☐	☐	☐	18.	☐	☐	☐	☐
4.	☐	☐	☐	☐	19.	☐	☐	☐	☐
5.	☐	☐	☐	☐	20.	☐	☐	☐	☐
6.	☐	☐	☐	☐	21.	☐	☐	☐	☐
7.	☐	☐	☐	☐	22.	☐	☐	☐	☐
8.	☐	☐	☐	☐	23.	☐	☐	☐	☐
9.	☐	☐	☐	☐	24.	☐	☐	☐	☐
10.	☐	☐	☐	☐	25.	☐	☐	☐	☐
11.	☐	☐	☐	☐	26.	☐	☐	☐	☐
12.	☐	☐	☐	☐	27.	☐	☐	☐	☐
13.	☐	☐	☐	☐	28.	☐	☐	☐	☐
14.	☐	☐	☐	☐	29.	☐	☐	☐	☐
15.	☐	☐	☐	☐	30.	☐	☐	☐	☐

Intermediate 2 Chemistry

| Practice Papers for SQA Exams | Time allowed: 2 hours | Exam 2 |

Fill in these boxes and read what is printed below.

Full name of school

Town

Forename(s)

Surname

Read each question carefully.

Attempt **all** questions.

Write your answers on the blank paper provided.

Write as neatly as possible.

Answer in sentences wherever possible.

Practice Papers for SQA Exams: Intermediate 2 Chemistry, Practice Exam 2

Read closely

1. For Section A, you should use an HB pencil and, where neccesary, a rubber.
2. Each answer is **either** A, B, C or D. When you have decided your answer, use your pencil to put a line in the appropriate space on the answer sheet. (See the example below.)
3. Each question has **only one correct** answer.
4. Do not do any rough working on the answer sheet: use a separate sheet of paper.

Sample question

The surface area:volume ratio of a cube with edges 1 cm is

A 1:1

B 3:1

C 6:1

D 12:1

The correct answer is **C** – 6:1. This answer has been clearly marked in **pencil** below.

Changing an answer

If you need to change an answer, carefully rub out your original, then use your pencil to fill in the answer you now want. Below, the answer has been changed to **D**.

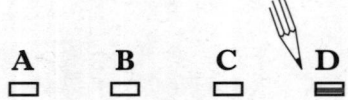

SECTION A

1. Which of the following elements is a halogen?

   A Bromine

   B Sodium

   C Neon

   D Magnesium

2. Which of the following is **not** an indication of a chemical reaction?

   A A gas being given off

   B A colour change

   C A solid dissolving

   D A precipitate being formed

3. Aluminium and magnesium both react with nitric acid. In which of the following would the reaction rate be slowest?

   A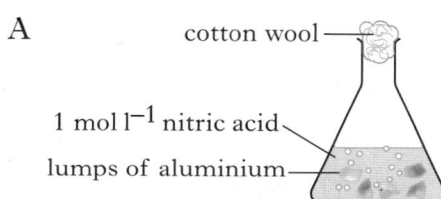

   B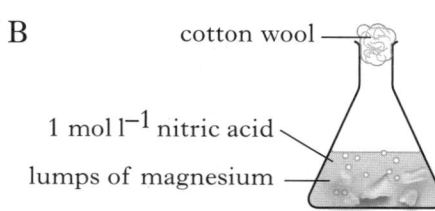

   C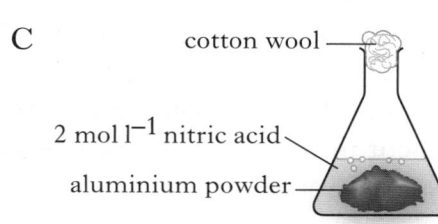

   D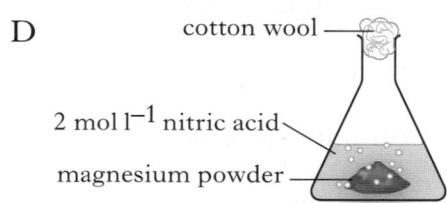

4. The course of a reaction was followed by measuring the volume of gas produced. 30 cm^3 of gas was collected after 120 s.

   What was the average rate of reaction in cm^3 s^{-1}?

   A 0·03

   B 0·25

   C 1

   D 4

5. Which of the following is the electron arrangement of a metal element?

   A 2, 8

   B 2, 8, 1

   C 2, 8, 7

   D 2, 8, 8

6. The diagram shown is representative of what type of structure?

   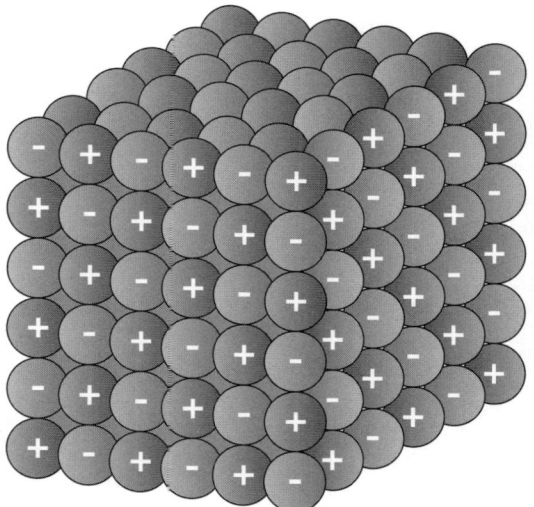

   A Covalent network

   B Covalent molecule

   C Ionic lattice

   D Metallic bonding

7. Which of the following compounds exists as discrete molecules?

   A Sulphur dioxide

   B Sodium chloride

   C Silicon dioxide

   D Silver(I) oxide

8. Which of the following elements can be described as monatomic?

   A Sulphur

   B Sodium

   C Helium

   D Hydrogen

9. An unknown element is found to have a melting point of over 2000°C but an oxide of this element is a gas at room temperature. What type of bonding will be present in the **element**?

   A Metallic

   B Pure covalent

   C Ionic

   D Polar covalent

10.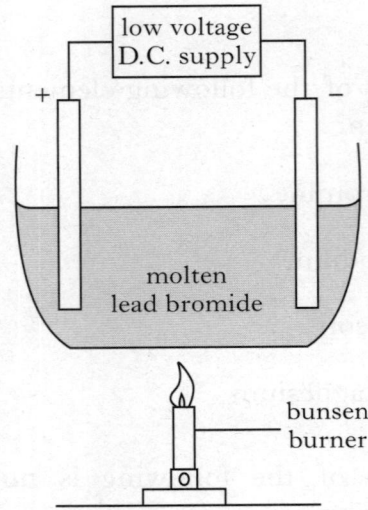

    During the electrolysis of molten lead bromide

    A lead atoms lose electrons to form ions

    B bromide ions lose electrons to form bromine molecules

    C lead atoms gain electrons to form lead ions

    D bromide ions gain electrons to form bromine molecules.

11. What is the name of the compound with the formula ZnO?

    A Zinc(I) oxide

    B Zinc(II) oxide

    C Zinc(III) oxide

    D Zinc(IV) oxide

12. Diesel cars do not use a spark to ignite the fuel. Which of the following compounds is **least** likely to be present in the exhaust emissions of a diesel powered car?

    A Carbon monoxide

    B Carbon dioxide

    C Sulphur dioxide

    D Nitrogen dioxide

13.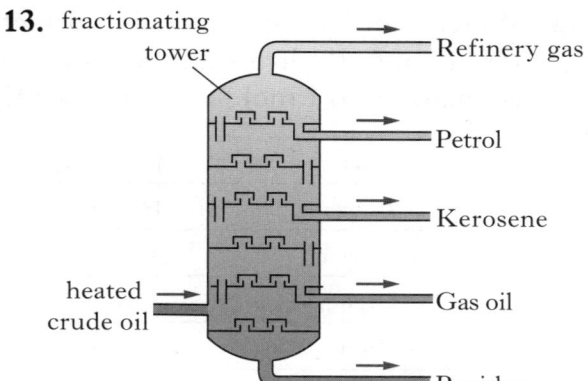

Fractional distillation produces several fractions. Which one of the fractions would be most likely to contain molecules with the formula C_8H_{18}?

A Refinery gas

B Petrol

C Kerosene

D Gas oil

14. The balanced equation for the complete combustion of a hydrocarbon **X** is shown below.

$$X(g) + 2O_2(g) \rightarrow CO_2(g) + 2H_2O(l)$$

Which of the following is the correct formula of hydrocarbon **X**?

A CH_4

B C_2H_6

C C_3H_8

D C_4H_{10}

15.

$$H-\underset{\underset{H}{|}}{\overset{\overset{H}{|}}{C}}-\underset{\underset{H}{|}}{\overset{}{C}}=\underset{}{\overset{}{C}}-\underset{\underset{H}{|}}{\overset{\overset{H}{|}}{C}}-\underset{\underset{H}{|}}{\overset{\overset{H}{|}}{C}}-H$$

The name of the above compound is

A prop-2-ene

B but-2-ene

C pent-2-ene

D pent-3-ene.

16. What is the correct systematic name for the following compound?

$$CH_3CHCHCH_2CH_2CH_3$$

A Hexane

B Hex-2-ene

C 2-methylpentane

D 3-methylpentane

17. What type of reaction is represented by the following equation?

$$C_2H_4 + H_2O \rightarrow C_2H_5OH$$

A Hydration

B Dehydration

C Hydrolysis

D Condensation

18. Which of the following can be classed as a carbohydrate?

A $C_6H_{13}OH$

B $C_6H_{12}O_2$

C $C_6H_{10}O_4$

D $C_6H_{12}O_6$

19. John was testing the carbohydrates, glucose, fructose and sucrose with Benedict's reagent. What line in the table shows the results that John can expect to find?

	Glucose	Fructose	Sucrose
A	No reaction	No reaction	No reaction
B	Blue → Orange	Blue → Orange	Blue → Orange
C	No reaction	No reaction	Blue → Orange
D	Blue → Orange	Blue → Orange	No reaction

20. Which of the following are naturally occurring esters?

A   Fats

B   Proteins

C   Starch

D   Carbohydrates

21. Which of the following solutions will produce a precipitate when mixed? (You may wish to use page 5 of the data booklet to help you.)

A   Sodium nitrate and nickel(II) chloride

B   Calcium bromide and sodium iodide

C   Lithium iodide and sodium carbonate

D   Sodium sulphate and barium nitrate

22. Which of the following oxides dissolves in water to produce an acidic solution?

A SO_2

B SiO_2

C SnO_2

D PbO_2

23. Which line in the table is correct for 1 mol l^{-1} hydrochloric acid in comparison to 1 mol l^{-1} ethanoic acid?

	pH	*Conductivity*
A	Lower	Higher
B	Lower	Lower
C	Higher	Lower
D	Higher	Higher

24. Which equation correctly shows the dissolving of ammonia in water?

A $NH_3(g) + H_2O(l) \rightarrow NH_4^+(aq) + OH^-(aq)$

B $NH_4^+(aq) + OH^-(aq) \rightarrow NH_3(g) + H_2O(l)$

C $NH_3(g) + H_2O(l) \rightleftharpoons NH_4^+(aq) + OH^-(aq)$

D $NH_4^+(aq) + OH^-(aq) \rightleftharpoons NH_3(g) + H_2O(l)$

25. Which of the following reactions can be classed as a redox reaction?

A   Displacement

B   Combustion

C   Precipitation

D   Fermentation

26. During the production of mercury from mercury(II) sulphide, mercury(II) ions are reduced. Which ion-electron equation below correctly shows this change?

A $Hg^+ + e^- \rightarrow Hg$

B $Hg \rightarrow Hg^+ + e^-$

C $Hg^{2+} + 2e^- \rightarrow Hg$

D $Hg \rightarrow Hg^{2+} + 2e^-$

27. Shown below is a simple cell.

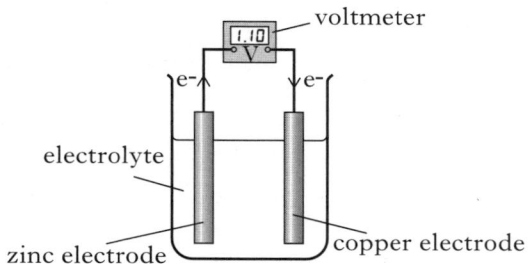

Which pair of metals would increase the value shown on the voltmeter?

A Magnesium and copper

B Iron and copper

C Zinc and iron

D Tin and copper

28. Experiments were performed on three unknown metal elements, X, Y and Z, to try to establish their reactivity. The results of the experiments are recorded in the table below.

Metal	Reaction with water	Reaction with dilute acid
X	No reaction	No reaction
Y	Slow reaction	Fast reaction
Z	No reaction	Slow reaction

The order of reactivity of the metals, starting with the **least** reactive, is

A Y, X, Z

B X, Z, Y

C Y, Z, X

D X, Y, Z

29. A sample of argon gas is contaminated with acidic hydrogen chloride. Which diagram shows the correct apparatus that could be used to remove the hydrogen chloride from the argon sample?

A
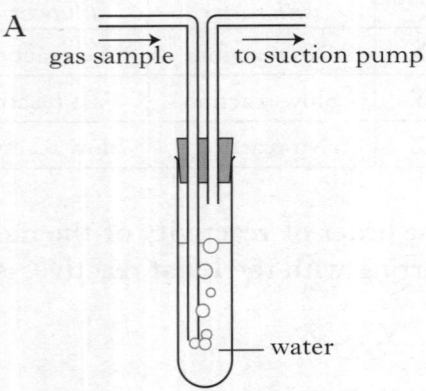

B
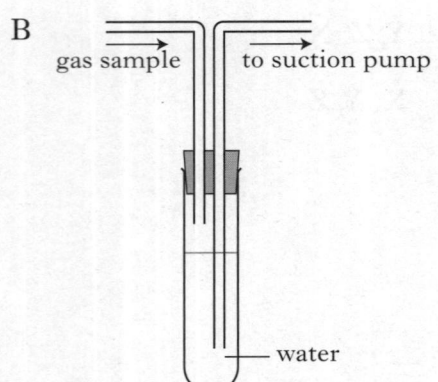

C
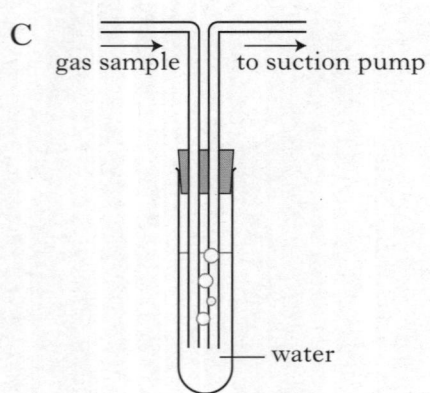

D
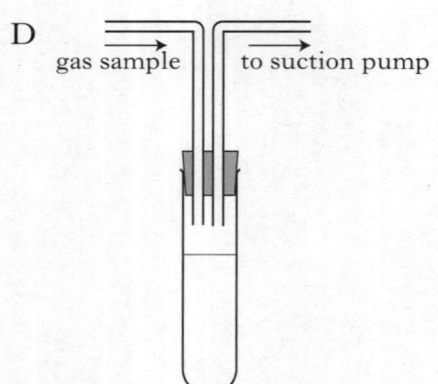

30. When iron corrodes, Fe^{2+} ions are formed. What indicator can be used to test for the presence of these ions?

A   Universal indicator

B   Ferroxyl indicator

C   Benedict's reagent

D   Bromine water

DO NOT WRITE IN THIS MARGIN

SECTION B

MARKS

1. (*a*) Nuclide notation can be used to show the numbers of protons, neutrons and electrons that an ion contains. The nuclide notation of a silver ion is shown.

$$^{107}_{47}Ag^{+}$$

Complete the table to show the number of each particle that this ion contains.

Particles	*Number*
Protons	
Electrons	
Neutrons	

2

(*b*) A sample of silver is found to contain two atoms of silver with different masses: ^{107}Ag and ^{109}Ag. What name is given to atoms with different masses?

______________________________________ 1

(*c*) The relative atomic mass of silver is 108. What does this suggest about the relative abundance of these different atoms?

______________________________________ 1

2. Magnesium metal reacts with hydrochloric acid to produce magnesium chloride and hydrogen gas.

(a) Write the balanced formula equation for this reaction.

(b) When the magnesium reacts with the acid, heat energy is released to the surroundings. What term is used to describe reactions that give out heat?

_____

(c) Complete the diagram showing how the hydrogen gas produced by this reaction could be collected.

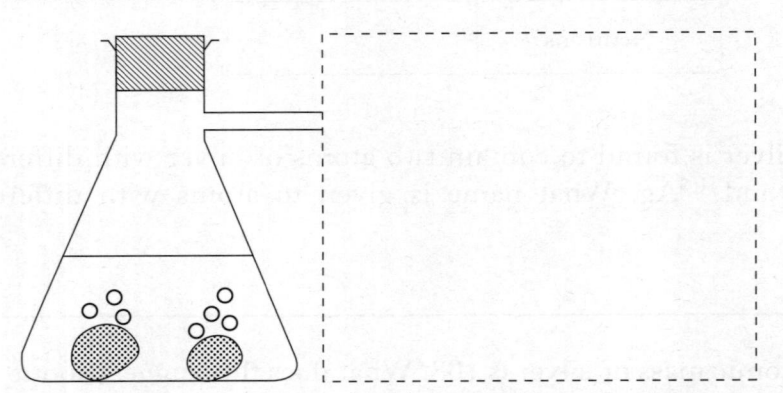

(d) The results of the experiment were recorded in the table below.

Time (min)	0	1	2	3	4	5	6	7	8
Volume of hydrogen (cm^3)	0	15	30	44	54	58	60	60	60

Draw a line graph of the results on the graph paper below.

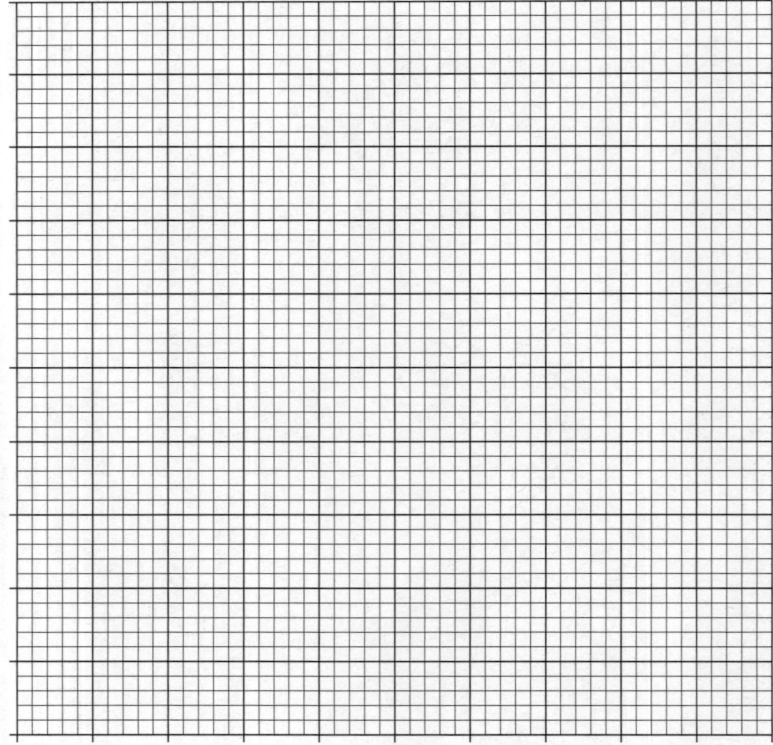

3. Iron is produced from iron ore in a blast furnace.

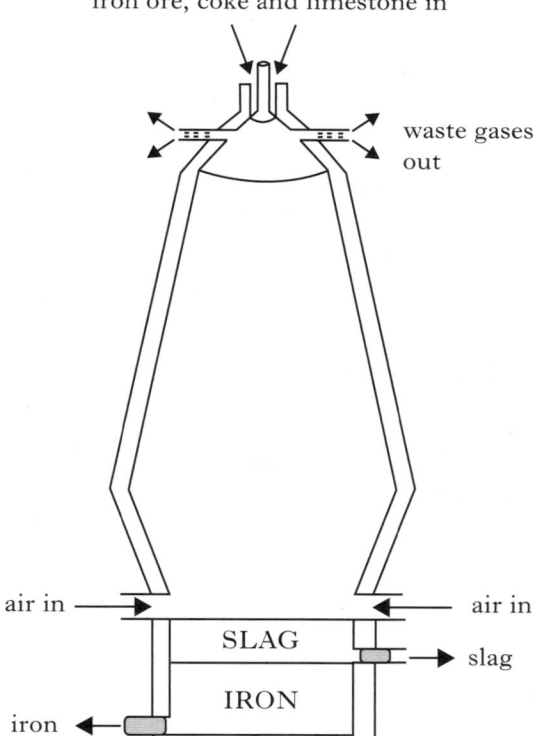

(a) When air is blown into the furnace, the temperature rises. Give a reason why air is blown into the blast furnace.

_____ 1

(b) The temperature of the blast furnace must never drop below 1600°C. Suggest the reason for this.

_____ 1

(c) One of the main reactions that take place in the blast furnace produces carbon monoxide gas.

$$2C(s) + CO_2(g) \rightarrow 2CO(g)$$

Calculate the mass of carbon monoxide produced when 132 kg of carbon dioxide reacts with excess carbon.

2

4. Magnesium metal can be extracted from seawater using electrolysis. Seawater contains about 0·13% magnesium. The flow diagram for this procedure is shown below.

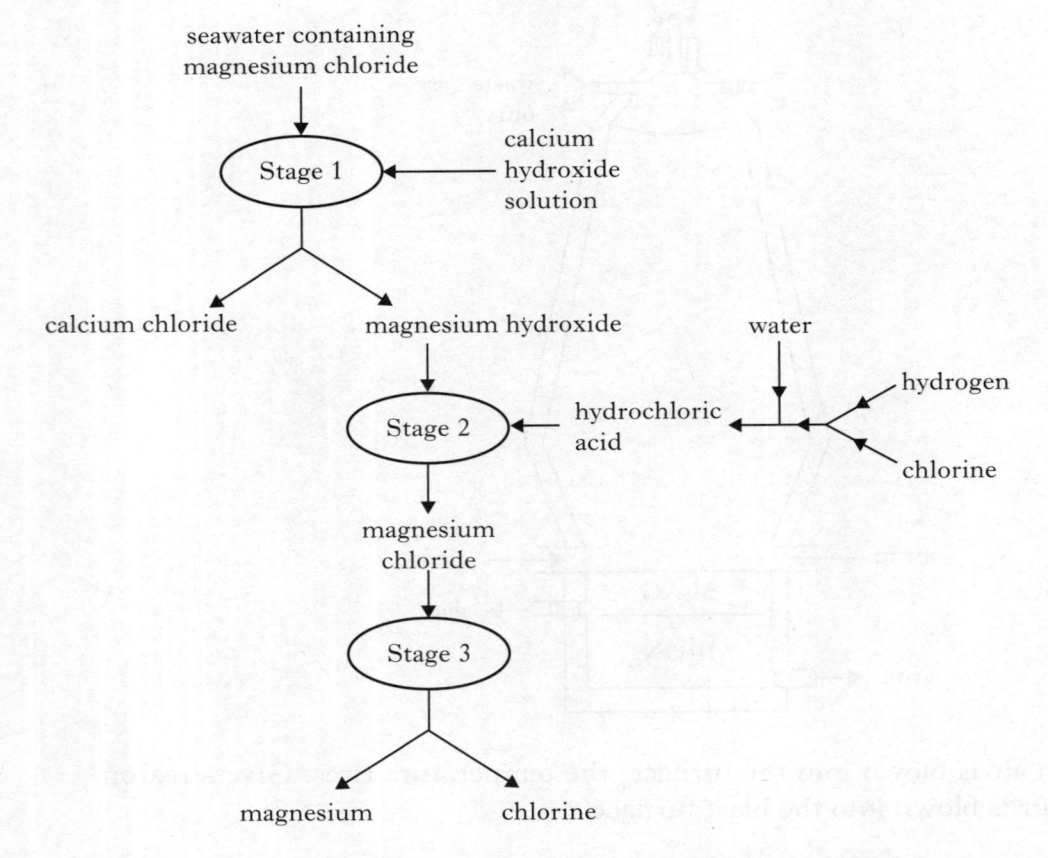

(a) Stages 1 and 2 involve chemical reactions. What name can be given to the reaction at stage 2?

_____ 1

(b) What process is taking place at stage 3 to separate the magnesium chloride into its constituent elements?

_____ 1

(c) Draw an arrow onto the diagram that would make the process more economical. 1

5. John added 5 g of chalk lumps to 50 cm³ of dilute hydrochloric acid. He noted the volume of carbon dioxide produced every ten seconds until the reaction was completed. The results of the experiment are shown on the graph below.

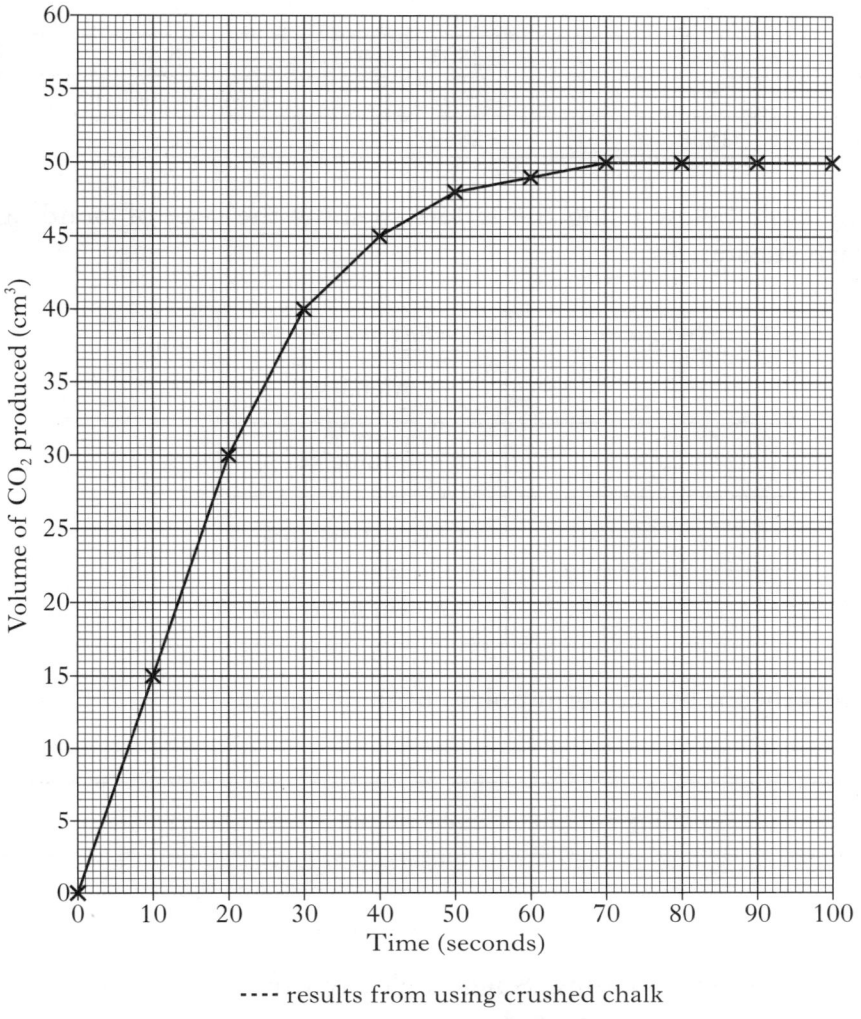

(graph: Volume of CO_2 produced (cm³) vs Time (seconds), showing chalk lumps curve passing through (0,0), (10,15), (20,30), (30,40), (40,45), (50,48), (60,49), (70,50), (80,50), (90,50), (100,50))

---- results from using crushed chalk
— results from using chalk lumps

(a) Calculate the average rate of reaction for the first 50 seconds.

_____

(b) John then repeated the experiment but used 5 g of crushed chalk with 50 cm³ of dilute hydrochloric acid. Draw a line on the graph to show the results that could John could have expected for this experiment.

_____

(c) Give a reason why the rate of both experiments slowed down as they proceeded.

_____

6. The properties of four different substances are shown in the table below.

Substance	Melting point (°C)	Boiling point (°C)	Conductor of electricity
A	−77	−33	No
B	1883	2503	No
C	773	1407	When molten
D	1538	2862	Yes

(a) Complete the table below using the letters to show the type of bonding present in each substance.

Substance	Bonding and structure
	Metallic
	Ionic
	Covalent network
	Covalent molecular

(b) Explain what is meant by the term polar covalent bond.

(c) Water has polar covalent bonding. Suggest clearly why water has a higher boiling point than might be expected.

7. A pupil was performing the PPA 'Testing for Unsaturation'. His results are recorded in the table below.

Hydrocarbon	Molecular formula	Observations on adding bromine solution	Saturated or unsaturated?
A	C_6H_{14}	Remains orange	Saturated
B	C_6H_{12}		Unsaturated
C	C_6H_{12}		Saturated
D	C_6H_{10}	Orange to colourless	Unsaturated

(a) Complete the table with the observations that you would expect to make regarding molecules B and C. **1**

(b) Draw the full structural formula of molecule B. **1**

(c) Molecules B and C have the same molecular formula but different structures. What name is given to two such molecules? **1**

_____

(d) State **two** safety precautions should be taken when performing this experiment. **1**

_____

8. Esters are sweet-smelling liquids that are widely used as flavourings in various foods. For example, the ester ethyl methanoate is added to sweets to give a raspberry flavour.

   (a) Draw the full structural formula of ethyl methanoate.

   1

   (b) Esters are produced by reacting an alkanol with an alkanoic acid. Name the alkanol that was used to produce ethyl methanoate.

   _____ 1

   (c) Name the type of reaction that occurs to produce an ester.

   _____ 1

9. Copper chloride can be separated into copper and chlorine gas by electrolysis.

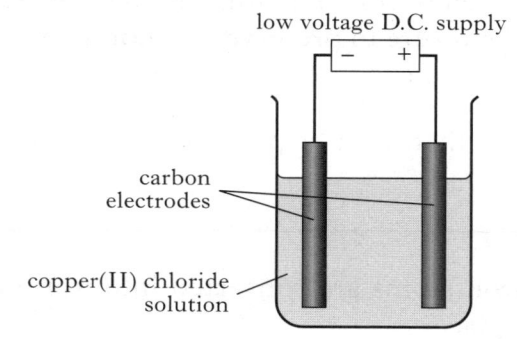

(a) During electrolysis a DC power supply must be used. Give the reason for this.

(b) The ion-electron equations taking place at the electrodes are:

$$Cu^{2+} + 2e^- \rightarrow Cu$$

$$2Cl^- \rightarrow Cl_2 + 2e^-$$

Combine the two ion-electron equations to give the balanced redox equation.

(c) Considering the information shown above, at which electrode would the chlorine gas be produced?

10. Corrosion of iron costs the UK billions of pounds every year. A Department of Transport report has shown that over half a billion pounds' worth of corrosion prevention is necessary in the future to preserve the motorway and trunk road system in England and Wales alone.

(a) Name the two substances that must be present for iron to rust.

_____ 1

(b) When iron rusts, the iron atoms are converted into iron ions. Name the type of reaction taking place.

_____ 1

(c) When iron is galvanised to prevent corrosion it is coated with which metal?

_____ 1

(d) One method of corrosion prevention is sacrificial protection. In which of the following experiments would the iron metal be protected from corrosion?

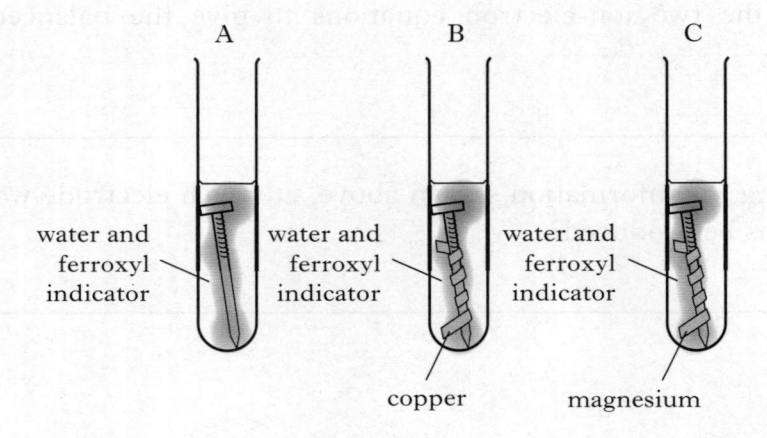

A — water and ferroxyl indicator
B — water and ferroxyl indicator, copper
C — water and ferroxyl indicator, magnesium

_____ 1

11. The aim of the PPA 'Reactions of Metals with Oxygen' is to place the metals copper, magnesium and zinc in order of reactivity. The following apparatus was used.

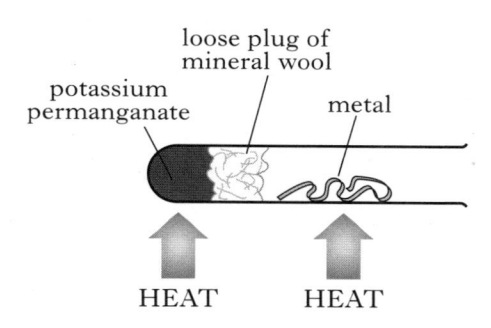

(diagram of test tube with potassium permanganate, loose plug of mineral wool, and metal, with HEAT arrows below)

(a) What is the purpose of the potassium permanganate?

_____ 1

(b) List the metals in order of reactivity from the most to the least reactive.

_____ 1

(c) Which of the metals would be extracted from its ore by electrolysis?

_____ 1

12. Farmer Lesley requires 2 mol l^{-1} potassium nitrate solution to test its effectiveness as a fertiliser on a new crop that she is producing. What mass of potassium nitrate is required to produce 1·5 l of this solution at this concentration?

2

13. Catalytic cracking is performed to break up long-chain hydrocarbons into smaller, more valuable molecules.

(a) Name a catalyst used to perform catalytic cracking in the lab.

_____

(b) Why is a catalyst used in this reaction?

_____

(c) Complete the equation below for the cracking of decane $C_{10}H_{22}$.

$$C_{10}H_{22} \rightarrow C_6H_{14} + \underline{\hspace{2cm}}$$

(d) One of the hydrocarbons produced by catalytic cracking is described as being unsaturated. What is meant by the term unsaturated?

_____

(e) What reagent can be used to distinguish between a saturated and an unsaturated hydrocarbon?

_____

14. Poly(ethenol) is a water-soluble plastic that has many uses, from laundry bags to dishwasher tablets.

(a) Plastics are synthetic. What is meant by the term synthetic?

_____

(b) When heated, poly(ethenol) softens and can be reshaped. What name is give to such plastics?

_____

Exam 3

Answer sheet for Section A:

Intermediate 2 Chemistry
Practice Papers for SQA Exams

Please select your answer using a single mark e.g. A ☐ B ▬ C ☐ D ☐

	A	B	C	D			A	B	C	D
1.	☐	☐	☐	☐		16.	☐	☐	☐	☐
2.	☐	☐	☐	☐		17.	☐	☐	☐	☐
3.	☐	☐	☐	☐		18.	☐	☐	☐	☐
4.	☐	☐	☐	☐		19.	☐	☐	☐	☐
5.	☐	☐	☐	☐		20.	☐	☐	☐	☐
6.	☐	☐	☐	☐		21.	☐	☐	☐	☐
7.	☐	☐	☐	☐		22.	☐	☐	☐	☐
8.	☐	☐	☐	☐		23.	☐	☐	☐	☐
9.	☐	☐	☐	☐		24.	☐	☐	☐	☐
10.	☐	☐	☐	☐		25.	☐	☐	☐	☐
11.	☐	☐	☐	☐		26.	☐	☐	☐	☐
12.	☐	☐	☐	☐		27.	☐	☐	☐	☐
13.	☐	☐	☐	☐		28.	☐	☐	☐	☐
14.	☐	☐	☐	☐		29.	☐	☐	☐	☐
15.	☐	☐	☐	☐		30.	☐	☐	☐	☐

Intermediate 2 Chemistry

| Practice Papers for SQA Exams | Time allowed: 2 hours | Exam 3 |

Fill in these boxes and read what is printed below.

Full name of school

Town

Forename(s)

Surname

Read each question carefully.

Attempt **all** questions.

Write your answers on the blank paper provided.

Write as neatly as possible.

Answer in sentences wherever possible.

Leckie × Leckie
Scotland's leading educational publishers

Read closely

1. For Section A, you should use an HB pencil and, where neccesary, a rubber.
2. Each answer is **either** A, B, C or D. When you have decided your answer, use your pencil to put a line in the appropriate space on the answer sheet. (See the example below.)
3. Each question has **only one correct** answer.
4. Do not do any rough working on the answer sheet: use a separate sheet of paper.

Sample question

The surface area:volume ratio of a cube with edges 1 cm is

A 1:1
B 3:1
C 6:1
D 12:1

The correct answer is **C** – 6:1. This answer has been clearly marked in **pencil** below.

Changing an answer

If you need to change an answer, carefully rub out your original, then use your pencil to fill in the answer you now want. Below, the answer has been changed to **D**.

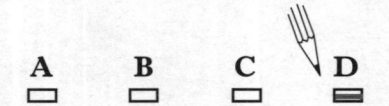

SECTION A

1. Which of the following elements has similar chemical properties to neon?

   A Sodium

   B Aluminium

   C Krypton

   D Fluorine

2. Which of the following compounds contains only two elements?

   A Sodium hydroxide

   B Sodium sulphate

   C Sodium sulphite

   D Sodium hydride

3. Experiment 1 on the graph below shows the volume of carbon dioxide gas collected when 1·0 g of chalk powder is reacted with an excess of 1 mol l^{-1} hydrochloric acid.

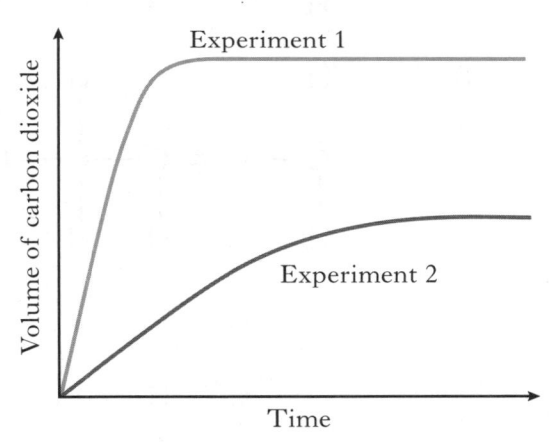

   Which of the following samples of chalk would produce the results shown for experiment 2?

   A 0·5 g of chalk lumps

   B 0·5 g of chalk powder

   C 1 g of chalk lumps

   D 1 g of chalk powder

4. Which of the following electron arrangements is that of an element which has similar chemical properties to potassium?

   A 2, 8, 1

   B 2, 8, 2

   C 2, 8, 3

   D 2, 8, 4

5. A heterogeneous catalyst works by

   A temporarily adsorbing the reactant molecules onto its active sites

   B permanently adsorbing the reactant molecules onto its active sites

   C aiding the combustion process

   D making the products more stable.

6. Different atoms of the same element have identical

   A mass numbers

   B atomic numbers

   C number of neutrons

   D nuclei

7. Which of the following compounds contains both a transition metal ion and a halide ion?

   A Sodium chloride

   B Iron oxide

   C Magnesium bromide

   D Cobalt fluoride

8. Which of the following has a covalent molecular structure?

   A Argon

   B Carbon dioxide

   C Calcium chloride

   D Silicon dioxide

9. All metals can conduct electricity because

   A the electricity breaks the bonds between the atoms

   B the outer energy level electrons in metals are free to move

   C the shared electrons between the atoms attract stray protons

   D the metals contain mobile ions.

10. Three moles of oxygen is mixed with two moles of methane gas and ignited. What is the correct balanced equation for this reaction?

    A $CH_4 + 2O_2 \rightarrow CO_2 + 2H_2O$

    B $2CH_4 + O_2 \rightarrow 2CO_2 + 2H_2O$

    C $3CH_4 + 6O_2 \rightarrow 3CO_2 + 6H_2O$

    D $3CH_4 + 2O_2 \rightarrow 3CO_2 + 6H_2O$

11. What name is given to the reaction shown by the following equation?

    $$C_2H_4 + H_2 \rightarrow C_2H_6$$

    A Combustion

    B Hydrolysis

    C Hydration

    D Addition

12. Listed below are some of the pollutants released by cars. Which one of these pollutants is **not** the result of incomplete combustion?

    A Carbon monoxide

    B Carbon

    C Nitrogen dioxide

    D Hydrocarbons

13. Which of the following is **not** an isomer of the structure shown below?

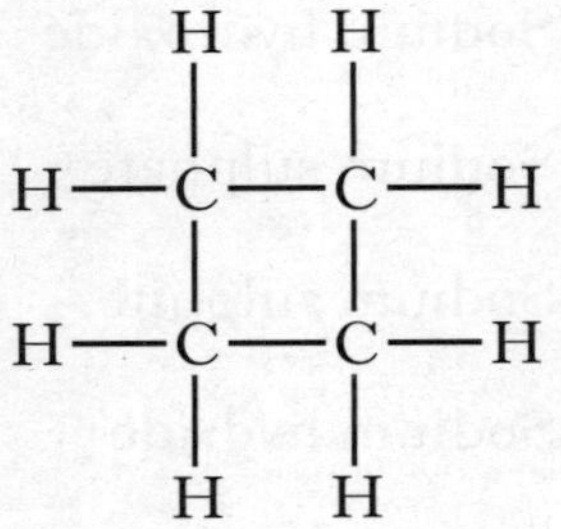

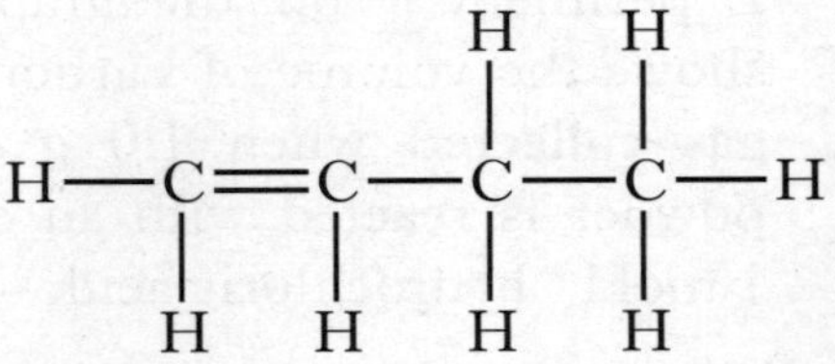

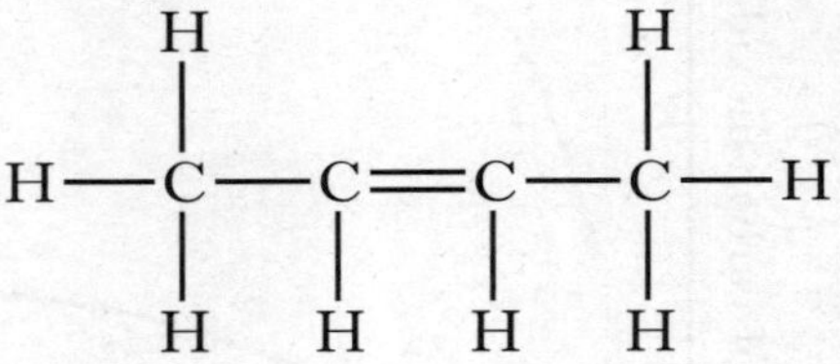

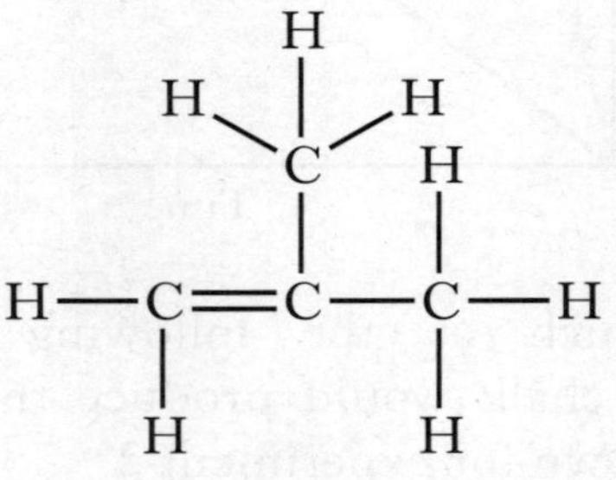

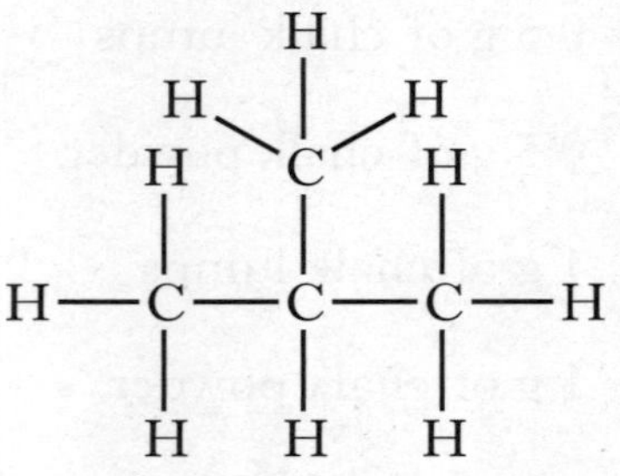

14. [structure shown]

The name of the above molecule is

A methyl ethanoate

B ethyl methanoate

C propanoic acid

D ethanoic acid

15. The flow diagram shows the manufacture of polymers from crude oil.

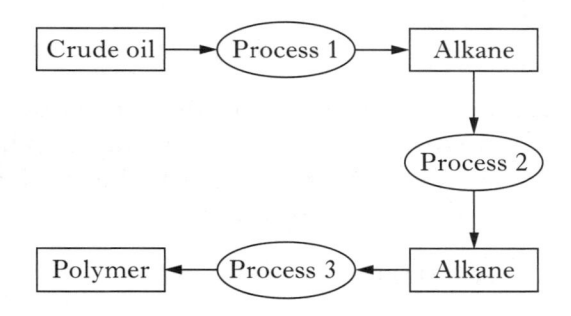

Crude oil → Process 1 → Alkane → Process 2 → Alkane → Process 3 → Polymer

Which line in the table correctly identifies processes 1, 2 and 3?

	Process 1	Process 2	Process 3
A	Polymerisation	Cracking	Distillation
B	Combustion	Distillation	Polymerisation
C	Distillation	Polymerisation	Combustion
D	Distillation	Cracking	Polymerisation

16. Which type of reaction converts ethanol to ethene?

A Dehydration

B Hydrolysis

C Condensation

D Dehydrogenation

17. Which of the following is a renewable energy source?

A Ethanol

B Oil

C Coal

D Natural gas

18. Which of the following compounds does **not** represent a carbohydrate?

A $C_{12}H_{22}O_{11}$

B $(C_6H_{10}O_5)_n$

C $C_3H_6O_2$

D $C_6H_{12}O_6$

19. What type of substance is formed when a protein is hydrolysed?

A Carbohydrate

B Ester

C Amino acid

D Fatty acid

20. During the formation of an ester, which two functional groups combine in the process?

A Hydroxyl and carbonyl

B Hydroxyl and carboxyl

C Amino and carboxyl

D Carbonyl and carboxyl

21. In the diagram below, what is the purpose of the ion bridge?

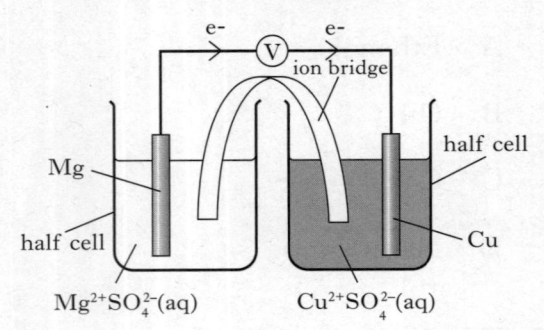

    A To complete the circuit
    B To provide ions
    C To indicate that a reaction has taken place
    D To act as a catalyst

22. Which of the following would **not** protect iron from corrosion?

    A Covering the iron in grease
    B Galvanising the iron
    C Wrapping a piece of magnesium wire round the iron
    D Wrapping a piece of copper wire round the iron

23. Which of the following ion-electron equations show iron(II) ions being oxidised?

    A $Fe(s) \rightarrow Fe^{2+}(aq) + 2e^-$
    B $Fe^{2+}(aq) + 2e^- \rightarrow Fe(s)$
    C $Fe^{2+}(aq) + 2e^- \rightarrow Fe^{3+}(aq)$
    D $Fe^{2+}(aq) \rightarrow Fe^{3+}(aq) + e^-$

24. An iron nail is placed in saltwater and ferroxyl indicator as shown.

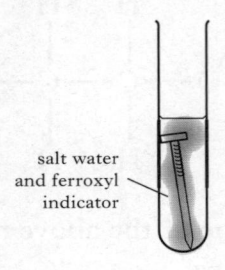

    After some time, a blue colour is visible around the nail and there is also a pink colour formed in the solution. Which ion is responsible for the pink colour?

    A Fe^{2+}
    B Fe^{3+}
    C OH^-
    D H^+

25. 0·3 moles of sodium hydroxide is dissolved in 100 cm³ of water. What is the concentration of the sodium hydroxide solution in mol l⁻¹?

    A 0·003
    B 0·03
    C 0·3
    D 3

26. Which of the following solutions has the lowest pH?

    A 1 mol l⁻¹ hydrochloric acid
    B 1 mol l⁻¹ ethanoic acid
    C 1 mol l⁻¹ ammonia solution
    D 1 mol l⁻¹ sodium hydroxide

27. An unknown white solid is soluble in water. The unknown solid also reacts with hydrochloric acid to produce carbon dioxide gas. The solid could be

    A   sodium oxide

    B   copper(II) carbonate

    C   aluminium oxide

    D   potassium carbonate.

28. Which of the following metals would react with dilute sulphuric acid to produce hydrogen gas?

    A   Gold

    B   Aluminium

    C   Mercury

    D   Copper

29. What type of reaction is represented by the equation shown?

    $Pb(NO_3)(aq) + 2NaI(aq) \rightarrow PbI_2(s) + 2NaNO_3(aq)$

    A   Neutralisation

    B   Precipitation

    C   Displacement

    D   Condensation

30. $H^+(aq) NO_3^-(aq) + K^+(aq) OH^-(aq) \rightarrow K^+(aq) NO_3^-(aq) + H_2O(l)$

    The spectator ions in the equation above are

    A $H^+(aq)$ and $K^+(aq)$

    B $H^+(aq)$ and $OH^-(aq)$

    C $K^+(aq)$ and $NO_3^-(aq)$

    D $K^+(aq)$ and $OH^-(aq)$

SECTION B

1. The structure of a fat molecule is shown

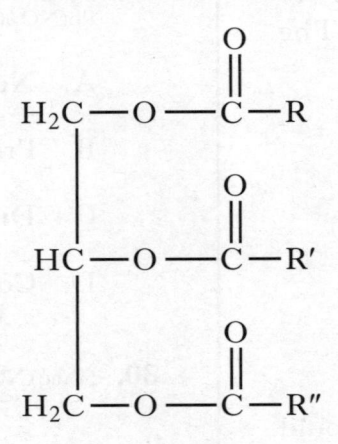

$$\begin{array}{c} H_2C-O-\overset{O}{\underset{\|}{C}}-R \\ HC-O-\overset{O}{\underset{\|}{C}}-R' \\ H_2C-O-\overset{O}{\underset{\|}{C}}-R'' \end{array}$$

(a) When the fat is hydrolysed fatty acids are obtained. The fatty acids are represented by R, R' and R" in the diagram. Name the other product of this reaction.

_____ 1

(b) Which have the higher melting point, fats or oils?

_____ 1

(c) Due to their functional group, fats and oils can be classified as what type of compound?

_____ 1

(d) Saturated fats have higher melting points than oils. What is meant by the term saturated?

_____ 1

2. A PPA experiment to study the effect of varying the concentration of sodium persulphate solution on its rate of reaction with potassium iodide was performed by students in the lab. They mixed 10 cm³ of sodium persulphate solution and 1 cm³ of starch solution, then added, using a syringe, 10 cm³ of potassium iodide solution. The time taken for the colour change to occur was recorded.

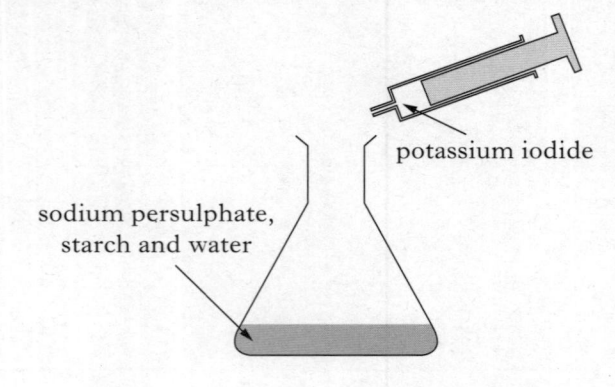

potassium iodide

sodium persulphate, starch and water

The experiment was repeated using different concentrations of sodium persulphate. The results table for the experiment has not been completed.

2. (continued)

(a) Complete the table of results by giving the values of **X** and **Y**.

Volume of sodium persulphate solution / cm³	Volume of water / cm³	Time / s	Relative rate / s⁻¹
10	0	X	0·0454
8	2	25	0·0400
6	4	33	Y
4	6	48	0·0208

(b) What colour change would indicate that the reaction had finished?

_____

(c) Draw a graph of the volume of sodium persulphate solution against the relative rate of reaction.

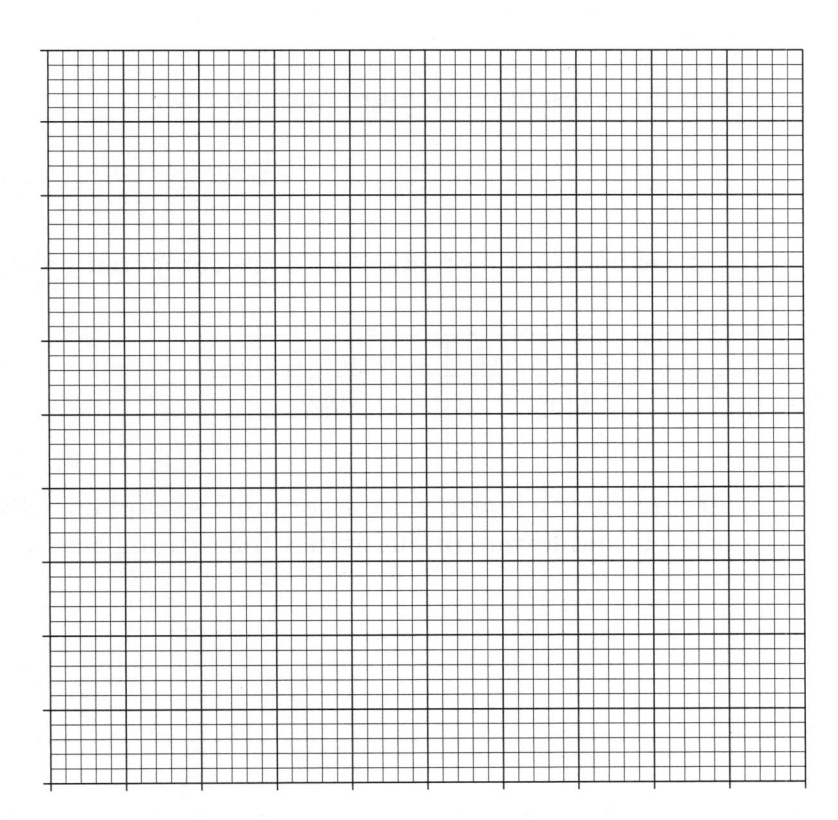

(d) The method of dilution of the sodium persulphate ensures that the total volume is kept constant. Why is this important in the experiment?

_____

3. Green salt (uranium tetrafluoride) is used to produce fuel for nuclear power stations. It is produced from uranium ore.

(a) Uranium can be extracted from green salt in a redox reaction with magnesium metal.

$$2Mg + UF_4 \rightarrow 2MgF_2 + U$$

Give another name for this type of reaction.

_____

(b) For this reaction to take place, the UF_4 must be in the molten state. Therefore the reaction is carried out at a temperature of over 1100°C. The reaction is carried out in an argon atmosphere. Give a reason why the reaction is not carried out in air.

_____

(c) Uranium hexafluoride can also be used as a fuel for nuclear power plants. Listed below are some of the properties of UF_6.

Properties of UF_6

Appearance	Colourless solid
Density	5·09 g/cm³
Melting point	64·8°C

Suggest the type of bonding present in uranium hexafluoride.

_____

4. The properties of hydrochloric acid and methanoic acid are compared in the table below

Property	Methanoic acid	Hydrochloric acid
Conductivity	Low	High
pH	4	1

(a) Using methanoic acid and hydrochloric acid as examples, explain why weak acids have higher pHs and lower conductivities than strong acids of the same concentration.

_____

_____

_____

(b) Write an equation for hydrogen chloride dissolving in water.

5. The diagram below shows two methods of hydrolysing starch. In both cases the starch undergoes a hydrolysis reaction to produce glucose.

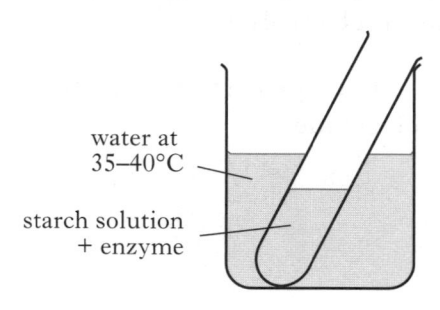

(a) Benedict's solution is added to each test tube at the end of the experiment. What colour change would take place?

_____ **1**

(b) When starch is hydrolysed using an acid, it is important to add sodium hydrogen carbonate to the test tube before the Benedict's solution is added. Give the reason for this.

_____ **1**

(c) Suggest why it is important to have a control test tube in each beaker that contains starch and water only.

_____

_____ **1**

6. Some sterilising pads contain a 65% solution of isopropyl alcohol in water. Isopropyl alcohol has the systematic name propan-2-ol.

(a) Draw the full structural formula of isopropyl alcohol.

1

(b) Name an isomer of propan-2-ol.

_____ **1**

(c) A typical sterilising pad contains approximately 0·6 g of propan-2-ol. How many moles of propan-2-ol does a typical sterilising pad contain?

2

7. In an experiment similar to the PPA 'Factors Affecting Voltage', a student investigated the effect that changing the metal electrodes had on the voltage produced by a cell when using sodium chloride as an electrolyte.

(a) Draw and label the cell which would be used to measure the voltage produced when zinc and iron are used as the electrodes.

1

(b) The results obtained by the student were recorded in the table below.

Electrodes	Reading on voltmeter (V)	Direction of electron flow
Zn/Fe	0·3	Zn → Fe
Zn/Al	−0·1	
Zn/Ni	0·5	Zn → Ni
Zn/Sn		Zn → Sn

Using the results obtained, complete the table by:

(i) Predicting the voltage that would be produced when tin is used with zinc as electrodes.

1

(ii) Predicting the direction of electron flow when aluminium is used as an electrode with zinc.

1

(c) Name **two** factors that should be kept constant throughout the experiment to ensure the results obtained are fair.

1

8. Octane number is a measure of how efficiently a fuel burns. A pupil was investigating the octane number of four different hydrocarbons. His results are recorded below.

Hydrocarbon	Molecular formula	Octane number
Hexane	C_6H_{14}	25
Heptane	C_7H_{16}	
2-methylpentane	C_6H_{14}	71
2-methylhexane	C_7H_{16}	47

(a) What conclusion can be drawn that links the structure of the hydrocarbon to its octane number?

(b) Predict the octane number of heptane.

(c) Hexane and 2-methylpentane have the same molecular formula but different structural formulae. What term can be used to describe this pair of hydrocarbons?

9. The concentration of ethanoic acid in vinegar can be calculated by neutralising a sample with 0·5 mol l⁻¹ sodium hydroxide solution.

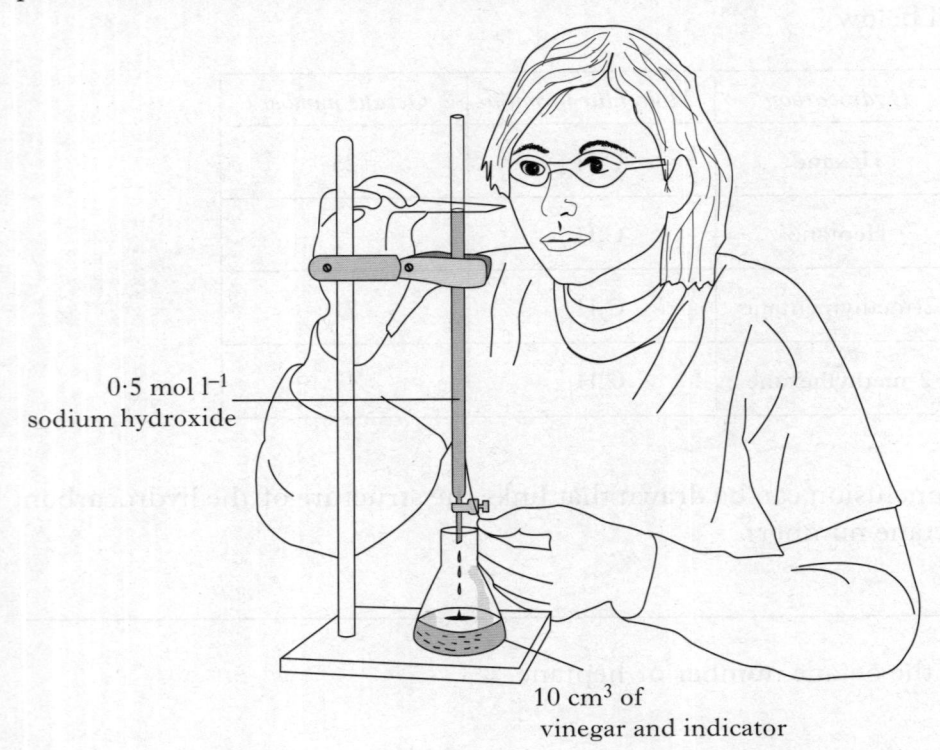

0·5 mol l⁻¹ sodium hydroxide

10 cm³ of vinegar and indicator

20 cm³ of sodium hydroxide was required to neutralise the vinegar. Calculate the concentration in mol l⁻¹ of the ethanoic acid in the vinegar.

2

10. The following experiment was performed in the lab to test the products of combustion of ethanol. The ethanol was burned in a spirit burner and the carbon dioxide produced was detected using limewater. The water produced in this reaction was also collected.

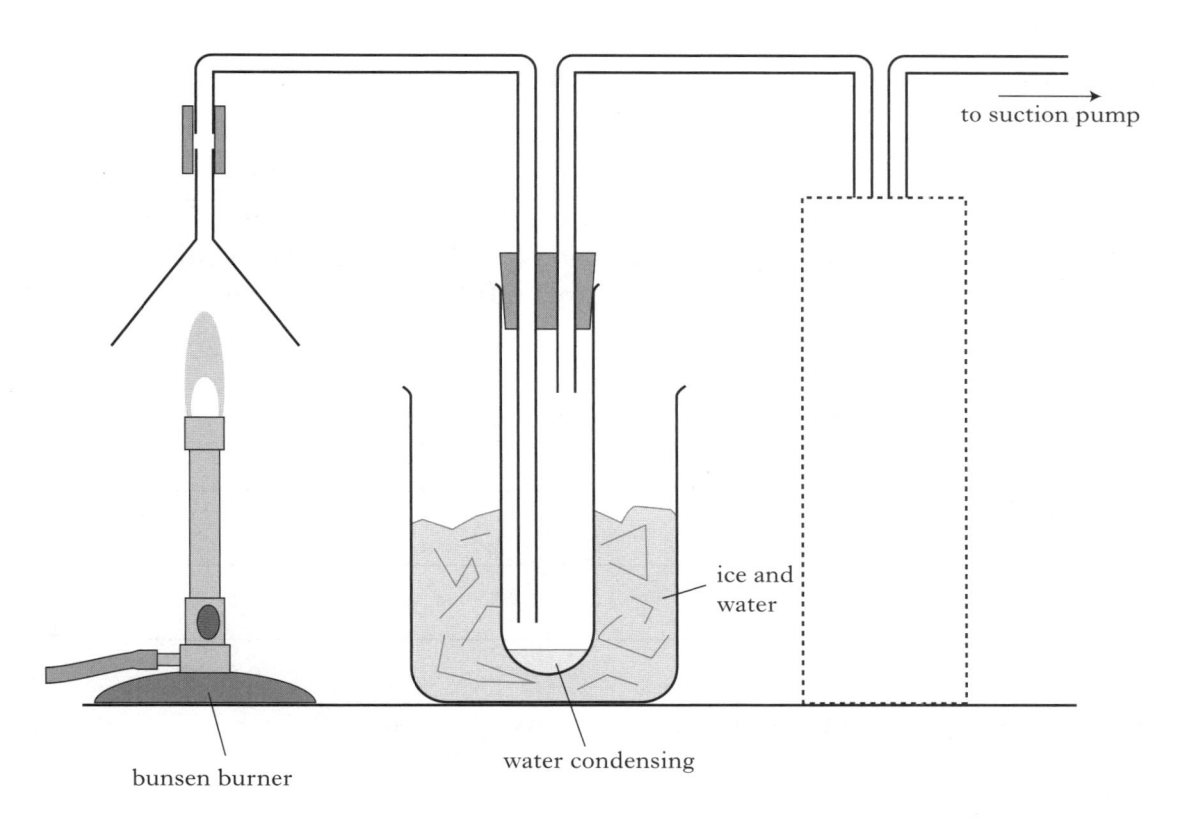

(a) Complete the diagram above showing the arrangement you would use to test for any carbon dioxide produced.

1

(b) What is the purpose of the iced water?

1

(c) After some time the funnel becomes covered in soot. Explain why this happens.

1

11. Steel can be protected from corrosion by coating it with zinc or tin.

(a) What name is given to the coating of steel with zinc?

(b) What two substances must reach the surface of the steel before corrosion can take place?

(c) Steel plant pots are protected from corrosion by coating them with either zinc or tin. If the plant pot is scratched, explain **fully** why the zinc coating would provide the better protection.

12. Copper is a very good conductor of both electricity and heat.

(a) Explain why metals such as copper can conduct electricity.

(b) Although copper is a fairly unreactive metal, it will still react with chlorine gas to produce copper(II) chloride. Write the balanced equation for this reaction.

(c) The chloride ions in copper(II) chloride have a stable electron arrangement. How do they achieve this?

(d) Copper(II) chloride can be separated by electrolysis. Write the ion-electron equation for the reaction that takes place at the negative electrode when a solution of copper(II) chloride is electrolysed.

DO NOT WRITE IN THIS MARGIN

MARKS

13. Styrene, which is also known as phenylethene, can be extracted from the sap of the styrax tree.

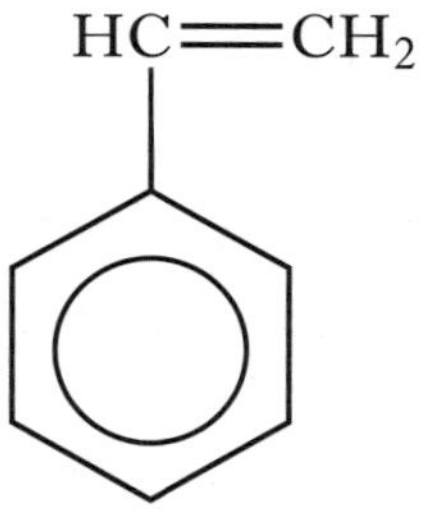

Styrene is the monomer used to produce polystyrene.

(*a*) Name the type of polymerisation that takes place to form polystyrene.

____ **1**

(*b*) Draw a section of the polystyrene polymer showing three monomer units combined.

1

(*c*) Polystyrene is classed as a thermoplastic. What is meant by the term thermoplastic?

____ **1**

14. Catalytic converters in car exhausts convert harmful gases into less harmful gases. Two of the less harmful gases formed are a result of a reaction between carbon monoxide and nitrogen monoxide.

(a) Name the two gases produced as a result of this reaction.

_____ 1

(b) Give a reason why carbon monoxide is produced in a car engine.

_____ 1

(c) Diesel cars do not produce nitrogen monoxide. Suggest a reason for this.

_____ 1

(d) The catalyst used in a car exhaust can be described as a heterogeneous catalyst. What is a heterogeneous catalyst?

_____ 1

Worked Answers

EXAM 1 — WORKED ANSWERS

SECTION A

Question	Answer	Hint
1	B	The periodic table on page 8 of your data booklet has the dates of discovery of all elements.
2	B	Pay close attention to the state symbols and read the question carefully because it mentions the states of lithium hydroxide, and the lithium and hydroxide ions.
3	D	The equation used to calculate average rate is: **average rate = change in concentration ÷ change in time** ($0.15 \div 20$).
4	D	This should be a straight forward question. Low temperature, low concentration and large particle size all result in a slow reaction.
5	B	Isotopes have the same atomic number but different mass number. The change in mass is due to the number of neutrons.
6	A	Note the word atom. In an atom the number of electrons is equal to the number of protons (the atomic number). In an ion they are different.
7	D	The clue is in the name – diatomic – 2 atoms. Nitrogen monoxide has the formula NO and therefore has two atoms per molecule. Sodium fluoride is ionic and therefore does not form molecules.
8	C	Chlorine has a valency of 1 and therefore titanium must have a valency of 3 to hold on to the three chlorine atoms. All metals have a positive charge so the answer is 3+.
9	A	Learn the definitions of all bond types. It is a regular question in exams.
10	C	Distillation and fractional distillation separate mixtures of liquids with different boiling points.
11	C	Petrol contains hydrocarbons with approximately 8 carbon atoms per molecule. (Octane)
12	B	It is important to learn all the covalent network substances – diamond, graphite, silicon dioxide and silicon carbide.
13	A	Hydrogenation (addition of hydrogen) reduces the number of double bonds and therefore increases the melting point.
14	B	Find the longest chain of carbons and number the branches to give the lowest numbers.
15	B	This is a tricky question. Write out the molecular formula of the three molecules and see which of the options gives you the correct formula for all three.
16	A	Learn all the types of reaction because they appear more than once in most exams. Ethanol can also be produced by fermentation.
17	D	The clue is in the name of the polymer.
18	D	To do this question correctly it is essential to draw out the full structural formulae of the compounds and count all the carbon and hydrogen atoms that they contain.
19	C	Learn all the types of reaction because they appear more than once in most exams.

SECTION A (continued)

Question	Answer	Hint
20	C	Only starch reacts with iodine. Glucose, fructose and maltose all turn Benedict's from blue to brick red. Sucrose has no effect on iodine or Benedict's.
21	B	The equation used to calculate concentration is: **concentration = number of moles ÷ volume in litres.** $(0{\cdot}25 \div 0{\cdot}5)$. To convert cm^3 into litres, divide by 1000. (500 cm$^3 \div 1000 = 0{\cdot}5$ l)
22	C	Sulphuric, hydrochloric and nitric are all strong acids and a concentration of $0{\cdot}01$ mol l^{-1} is a dilute solution (low concentration).
23	A	**OIL RIG (oxidation is loss – reduction is gain.)** The copper(II) ions are gaining one electron so it is the reduction of Cu^{2+} ions.
24	B	Oxides are not salts and hydrogen chloride is better known as hydrochloric acid.
25	D	Identify the salt that is insoluble by using your data book.
26	B	Sulphur dioxide contributes to acid rain and is therefore an acidic gas that will react with an alkaline solution.
27	A	Electrons flow from the more reactive to the less reactive metal.
28	A	When iron corrodes it is oxidised (OIL RIG). The negative terminal supplies electrons to the iron which prevents the iron losing electrons required for it to corrode.
29	A	A metal will displace the ions of a less reactive metal from solution. Zinc is more reactive than iron but less reactive than magnesium.
30	C	Reactive metals, i.e. potassium to aluminium, are extracted from their ores by electrolysis.

Practice Papers for SQA Exams: Intermediate 2 Chemistry Answers to Exam 1

SECTION B

Question	Answer	Hint
1(a)	A covalent bond is a shared pair of electrons between two non-metals. The electrons are electrostatically attracted to the positive nuclei of the atoms.	Give as much detail as you can in this type of question to try to impress the examiner. But be careful not to include any incorrect information in your answer.
1(b)	H—C(—H)(—H)(—H) (tetrahedral structure)	Study how to draw the shape of both tetrahedral and pyramidal molecules because questions about them are common.
1(c)	A molecule is made up of two or more atoms covalently bonded.	
2(a)	$^{23}_{11}Na$	Atomic number is always at the bottom and mass number is always at the top.
2(b)	12	The number of neutrons is equal to the mass number minus atomic number.
2(c)	There is the same number of protons as electrons in each isotope, i.e. the proton to electron ratio is 1:1.	Atoms are electrically neutral because they have the same number of positive protons as negative electrons.
3(a)	(transition) metal	Read the question carefully. If you wrote platinum then you must pay more attention to the bold word in the question.
3(b)	A catalyst that is in a different state to the reactants.	You should also be able to describe how a heterogeneous catalyst works.
3(c)	$2NO(g) + O_2(g) \rightleftharpoons 2NO_2(g)$	Balancing equations can be tricky so practice as many as you can before the exam.
4(a)	A family of compounds with similar chemical properties that can be represented by a general formula.	Learn all the homologous series and their functional groups.
4(b)	CH_2O	This should be a straightforward question to answer.
4(c)	Carbon dioxide and water	When a substance burns, an oxide of each element in the substance is produced. The question asks for the products of complete combustion so no carbon monoxide will be produced.

Page 73

SECTION B (continued)

Question	Answer	Hint
5(a)	$MgCO_3 + H_2SO_4 \rightarrow MgSO_4 + CO_2 + H_2O$	It is important to learn the formulae of sulphuric acid (H_2SO_4), nitric acid (HNO_3) and hydrochloric acid (HCl). It is also important to learn the reactions of acids. acid + metal $\rightarrow$ salt + hydrogen acid + alkali $\rightarrow$ salt + water acid + base $\rightarrow$ salt + water acid + carbonate $\rightarrow$ salt + water + carbon dioxide
5(b)	(Diagram: filter funnel with excess magnesium or magnesium carbonate, filtering into magnesium sulphate solution)	When drawing diagrams, ensure that they are large, clear and well labelled. Examiners judge the diagram using the question 'Would the experiment work as drawn?' So it is important to draw it exactly as you should perform the experiment in the lab.
5(c)	When no more bubbles are produced or when there is magnesium carbonate left over and not reacting.	The acid would also be neutralised: this could be checked with pH paper.
5(d)	To ensure that all the sulphuric acid has been neutralised.	This is a PPA question. In each exam you will be questioned on two of the PPAs. To ensure that you have practiced fully for the exam, I have covered all nine of the PPAs in the three papers. This question is based on the PPA 'Preparation of a Salt' from unit 3.
6(a)	(Diagram: test tube with mineral wool soaked in liquid paraffin, catalyst, HEAT arrows, delivery tube leading to bromine solution)	This question is based on the PPA 'Cracking' from unit 2

Page 74

Practice Papers for SQA Exams: Intermediate 2 Chemistry Answers to Exam 1

SECTION B (continued)

Question	Answer	Hint
6(b)	The test tube of bromine water must be removed <u>before</u> the heat is removed.	You were no doubt reminded of this many times whilst carrying out this PPA!
6(c)	$C_{12}H_{26} \rightarrow C_8H_{18} + C_4H_8$	It is simple maths. Subtract the C_8H_{18} from the $C_{12}H_{26}$. The answer is C_4H_8.
6(d)	There are not enough hydrogen atoms for complete saturation.	
7(a)	The time taken for the cross to disappear.	This question is based on the PPA 'The effect of temperature changes on reaction rate'.
7(b)	0.0833 s^{-1}	In question 3 in section A you were asked to calculate the <u>average</u> rate. This question asks you to calculate the rate. Rate = 1 ÷ time (1 ÷ 12).
7(c)	The higher the temperature, the faster the reaction.	Easy! Not all the questions are hard.
8(a)	Neutralisation	I hope that you learned the equations in answer 5(a).
8(b)	105·49 g	Top tip for questions involving calculations based on balanced equations: **Never** use the reactant that is in excess in your calculation. Step 1 Work out the formula mass (FM) of iron(II) oxide using its formula. FeO = 1 × Fe(56) + 1 × O(16) = 56 + 16 = 72 g Step 2 Calculate the number of moles of FeO used using moles = mass ÷ FM (50 ÷ 72 = 0·694 moles) (1 mark) Step 3 The molar ratio can be established using the balanced equation. 1 mole of FeO produces 1 mole of FeSO$_4$. This means that if 0·69 moles of FeO was used, 0·69 moles of FeSO$_4$ will be produced. Step 3 Calculate the mass of FeSO$_4$ produced using mass = moles × FM (0·694 × 152 = 105·49 g). 152 is the formula mass of FeSO$_4$. Use the same method used in step 2 to calculate this. (1 mark)

SECTION B (continued)

Question	Answer	Hint
9(a)	Nitrogen from air + Hydrogen from methane → Compressor → Iron catalyst at 500°C → Condenser → Ammonia	Flow diagrams can seem complicated but the answers are given to you in the text at the start of the question. You just have to read the question carefully.
9(b)	Nitrogen from air + Hydrogen from methane → Compressor → Iron catalyst at 500°C → Condenser → Ammonia (with recycle loop from Condenser back to Iron catalyst)	The arrow shows that the unreacted nitrogen and hydrogen are removed from the condenser and put back into the reaction chamber.
9(c)	A weak alkali dissociates partially in solution.	The definitions of strong and weak are the same for acids and alkalis.

SECTION B (continued)

Question	Answer	Hint
9(d)	NaOH(s) → Na$^+$(aq) + OH$^-$(aq)	Strong acids and alkalis dissociate completely in solution. This is shown by the single arrow. Weak acids and alkalis dissociate partially. They would have a reversible arrow in their equations.
10(a)	It is lightweight / low density.	Learn the properties of the following recently developed plastics as they appear regularly in exams: poly(ethenol), Kevlar, biopol, poly(vinylcarbazole), poly(ethyne), low density poly(ethene)
10(b)	Amine group	It is essential to learn all the homologous series and their functional groups.
10(c)	Condensation polymerisation	Condensation polymerisation is the reaction in which many monomers combine to form a polymer with the elimination of **small** molecule. That small molecule, however, isn't necessarily water; in this case it is hydrogen chloride.
11(a)	H—C(=O)—O—H	It is essential to learn all the homologous series and their functional groups. When drawing structural formulae, always check that each element in the compound has the correct number of bonds i.e. Carbon = 4 bonds, and Hydrogen = 1 bond.
11(b)	Ethanol	When naming esters, the alcohol used goes to the front part of the name and the carboxylic acid used goes to the back of the name. **ester = alcohol to front, acid to back**
11(c)	Clear labelled diagram showing a water bath and paper towel condenser around the test tube; and concentrated sulphuric acid catalyst must be mentioned and mention of sodium hydrogen carbonate solution to neutralise the acid at the end of the reaction. Labels: paper towel soaked in cold water; hot water; alcohol and carboxylic acid plus a few drops of concentrated sulphuric acid	When drawing diagrams ensure that they are large, clear and well labelled. Examiners judge the diagram using the question 'Would the experiment work as drawn?' So it is important to draw it exactly as you should perform the experiment in the lab.

Practice Papers for SQA Exams: Intermediate 2 Chemistry Answers to Exam 1

SECTION B (continued)

Question	Answer	Hint
11(d)	No naked flames	A water bath must be used to heat the flammable liquids used in this experiment.
11(e)	Structure showing H–C(=O)–O–CH₃ (methyl formate): H-C with double bond to O, single bond to O-C-H with three H's	Always check that each carbon atom forms four bonds.
12(a)	Table: Sodium chloride — **Ionic** — Non-conductor — **Solid** Sodium — Metallic — Conductor — Solid Chlorine — Covalent — **Non-conductor** — Gas Carbon (graphite) — **Covalent** — Conductor — Solid 1 mark for each correct line in the table	It is vitally important to learn the various types of bonds and the properties of the substances that have these bonds. List all the type of bonds in a table and their properties in a table, then learn them because they will be in the exam.
13(a)	Displacement reaction or redox reaction	Learn the different types of reaction because they appear more than once in most exams.
13(b)	Nitrate ion	Spectator ions are unchanged by the reaction. They must appear on both sides completely unchanged, including what state they are.
13(c)	Silver is less reactive than copper.	This should be a fairly straight forward question. A metal will displace the ions of a less reactive metal from solution.
13(d)	$Cu(s) \rightarrow Cu^{2+}(aq) + 2e^-$	**OIL RIG.** The more reactive metal loses electrons, i.e. it is oxidised.

SECTION B (continued)

Question	Answer	Hint
14	20 g	Top tip for questions involving n = C × V: The volume must be in **litres**. Change cm³ into litres by dividing by 1000. **Step 1** Calculate the number of moles of acid required using n = C × V (2 × 0·25 = 0·5 moles) (1 mark) **Step 2** Work out the formula mass (FM) of sodium hydroxide using its formula. NaOH = 1 × Na (23) + 1 × O(16) + 1 × H(1) = 23 + 16 + 1 = 40 g **Step 3** Calculate the mass of NaOH required using mass = moles × FM (0·5 × 40 = 20 g) (1 mark)

EXAM 2 — WORKED ANSWERS

Section A

Question	Answer	Hint
1	A	A straightforward one to get you started.
2	C	There are only four indicators of reaction: colour change, gas evolved, energy change and precipitate formed.
3	A	Three factors – Al being less reactive than Mg, low concentration and large particle size – result in a slow reaction.
4	B	The equation used to calculate average rate is: **average rate = change in volume ÷ change in time** $(30 \div 120)$.
5	B	The group 1 (alkali metals) elements all have an electron arrangement that has 1 outer electron.
6	C	Learn the properties of covalent networks, ionic, covalent molecular and metallic substances.
7	A	You should be able to give examples of covalent networks, ionic, covalent molecular and metallic substances.
8	C	The noble gases can be described as monatomic because they don't form bonds and therefore they exist as single atoms.
9	B	Learn the properties of covalent networks, ionic, covalent molecular and metallic substances.
10	B	During electrolysis the non-metal ions will lose electrons and the metal ions will gain electrons to form atoms.
11	B	Oxygen has a valency of two; this means that it forms two bonds. If it is only holding onto one zinc atom, then zinc must also have a valency of two. The last three questions all have the answer B. However please remember that there is no pattern to answers but you will not get more than three of the same answers in a row.
12	D	Nitrogen dioxide is produced by sparking air. Diesel engines do not have spark plugs and therefore they don't produce nitrogen dioxide.
13	B	Petrol is mainly made of hydrocarbons with approximately 8 carbons atoms per molecule.
14	A	**Don't panic!** This question is not as hard as it seems. The equation is balanced, which means that **X** must contain only 1 carbon atom because there is only 1 carbon atom on the right-hand side of the equation.
15	C	If you selected D, then you must remember that when naming you should always check that the position of the functional group has the lowest possible number.
16	B	If you draw out the full structural formulae, these types of questions can seem slightly easier.
17	A	Learn all the types of reaction because they appear more than once in most exams.
18	D	Learn the formulae of the monosaccharides $(C_6H_{12}O_6)$, disaccharides $(C_{12}H_{22}O_{11})$, and polysaccharides $(C_6H_{10}O_5)_n$.
19	D	Sucrose does not react with Benedict's (or iodine). Glucose and fructose (and maltose) all react with Benedict's, turning it from blue to orange (brick red).
20	A	A common question. Remember it!

Section A (continued)

Question	Answer	Hint
21	D	A precipitate is an insoluble solid. When mixed, D would produce sodium nitrate (very soluble) and barium sulphate (insoluble). Barium sulphate is the precipitate.
22	A	Non-metal oxides dissolve in water to produce acid solutions. You may also have known this because sulphur dioxide contributes to acid rain.
23	A	Weak acids have high pHs and low conductivities because they have fewer ions in solution than strong acids, which have low pHs and high conductivities.
24	C	**Weak alkalis such as ammonia only dissociate partially** and therefore the equation must have an equilibrium (reversible) arrow to represent this.
25	A	All displacement reactions can be classed as redox reactions.
26	C	Reduction involves the gain of electrons and, because it was mercury(II) sulphate, the mercury ions would have a charge of 2+.
27	A	The further apart the metals are in the electrochemical series, the higher the voltage will be.
28	B	This question requires some time and careful thinking because it can be easy to make mistakes.
29	A	The experiment would only work as drawn in A. The delivery tube must bubble the gas into the water to dissolve the acid gas. The insoluble argon would then leave through the shorter tube.
30	B	Ferroxyl indicator turns blue with Fe^{2+} ions. It turns pink with OH^- ions.

Section B

Question	Answer	Hint
1(a)	<table><tr><th>Particles</th><th>Number</th></tr><tr><td>Protons</td><td>47</td></tr><tr><td>Electrons</td><td>46</td></tr><tr><td>Neutrons</td><td>60</td></tr></table>	The number of protons is equal to the atomic number = 47. The ion has a charge of 1+. This means that it has 1 more positive proton than negative electrons so there must be 46 electrons. The number of neutrons is equal to the mass number minus the atomic number. (107 − 47 = 60)
1(b)	Isotopes	Isotopes have the same atomic number but different mass numbers. Isotopes have different number of neutrons.
1(c)	It suggests that there are equal amounts of each isotope.	The relative atomic mass is the average mass of all the isotopes of an element. This means that the mass will be closest to the most abundant isotope (the mass of the most common isotope). In this case, the mass is exactly between the two isotopes which means there are equal amounts of each isotope.
2(a)	$2HCl + Mg \rightarrow MgCl_2 + H_2$	It is important to learn all the reactions involving acids: acid + alkali → salt + water acid + metal → salt + hydrogen acid + carbonate → salt + water + carbon dioxide acid + base → salt + water In this question you get 1 mark for the correct equation and 1 mark for balancing it correctly.
2(b)	Exothermic reaction	Exothermic reactions release heat to the surroundings.
2(c)	(diagram: gas collection over water — H_2 collected in inverted measuring cylinder over water, connected to flask containing magnesium and hydrochloric acid(aq))	Collecting a gas by this method is commonly asked about. Ensure the diagram you draw is clear and labelled.

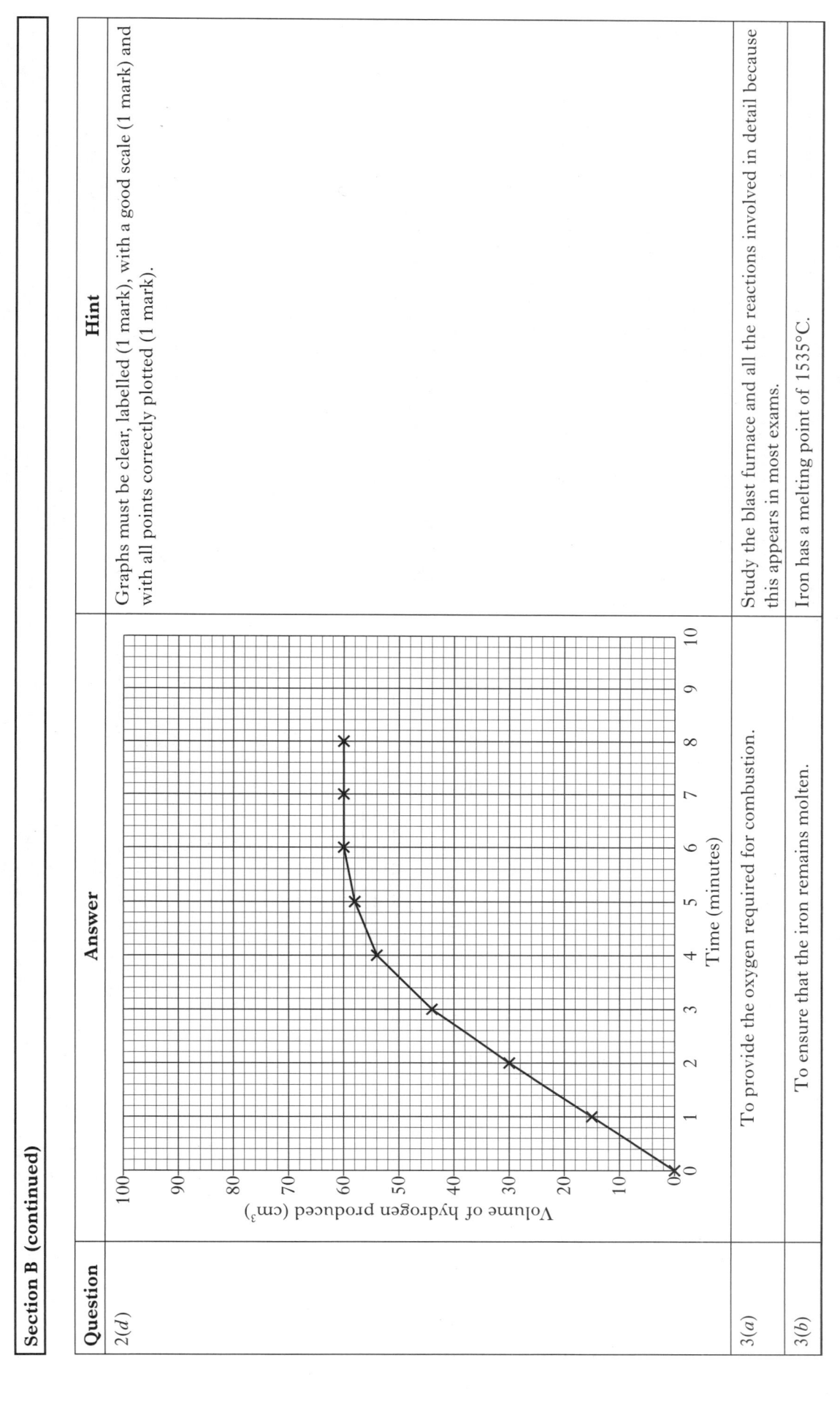

Section B (continued)

Question	Answer	Hint
2(d)	[Graph: Volume of hydrogen produced (cm³) vs Time (minutes). Points plotted at approximately (0,0), (1,15), (2,30), (3,45), (4,54), (5,58), (6,60), (7,60), (8,60)]	Graphs must be clear, labelled (1 mark), with a good scale (1 mark) and with all points correctly plotted (1 mark).
3(a)	To provide the oxygen required for combustion.	Study the blast furnace and all the reactions involved in detail because this appears in most exams.
3(b)	To ensure that the iron remains molten.	Iron has a melting point of 1535°C.

Section B (continued)

Question	Answer	Hint
3(c)	168 kg	This is similar to question 8(b) section B in practice paper 1. Top tip for questions involving calculations based on balanced equations: **Never** use the reactant that is in excess in your calculation. Step 1 Work out the formula mass (FM) of carbon dioxide using its formula. $CO_2 = 1 \times C(12) + 2 \times O(16) = 12 + 32 = 44$ g Step 2 Calculate the number of moles of CO_2 used using moles = mass ÷ FM (132 ÷ 44 = 3 moles) (1 mark) Step 3 The molar ratio can be established using the balanced equation. 1 mole of CO_2 produces 2 mole of CO. This means that if 3 moles of CO_2 was used, 6 moles of CO will be produced. Step 4 Calculate the mass of CO produced using mass = moles × FM (6 × 28 = 168 kg). 28 is the formula mass of CO. Use the same method used in step 2 to calculate this. (1 mark)
4(a)	Neutralisation	Questions involving flow diagrams are always difficult and require a lot of thinking to answer correctly. Try writing out the equation for the reaction taking place. It may make the answer easier to find.
4(b)	Electrolysis	Electrolysis is used to break up ionic compounds.

Section B (continued)

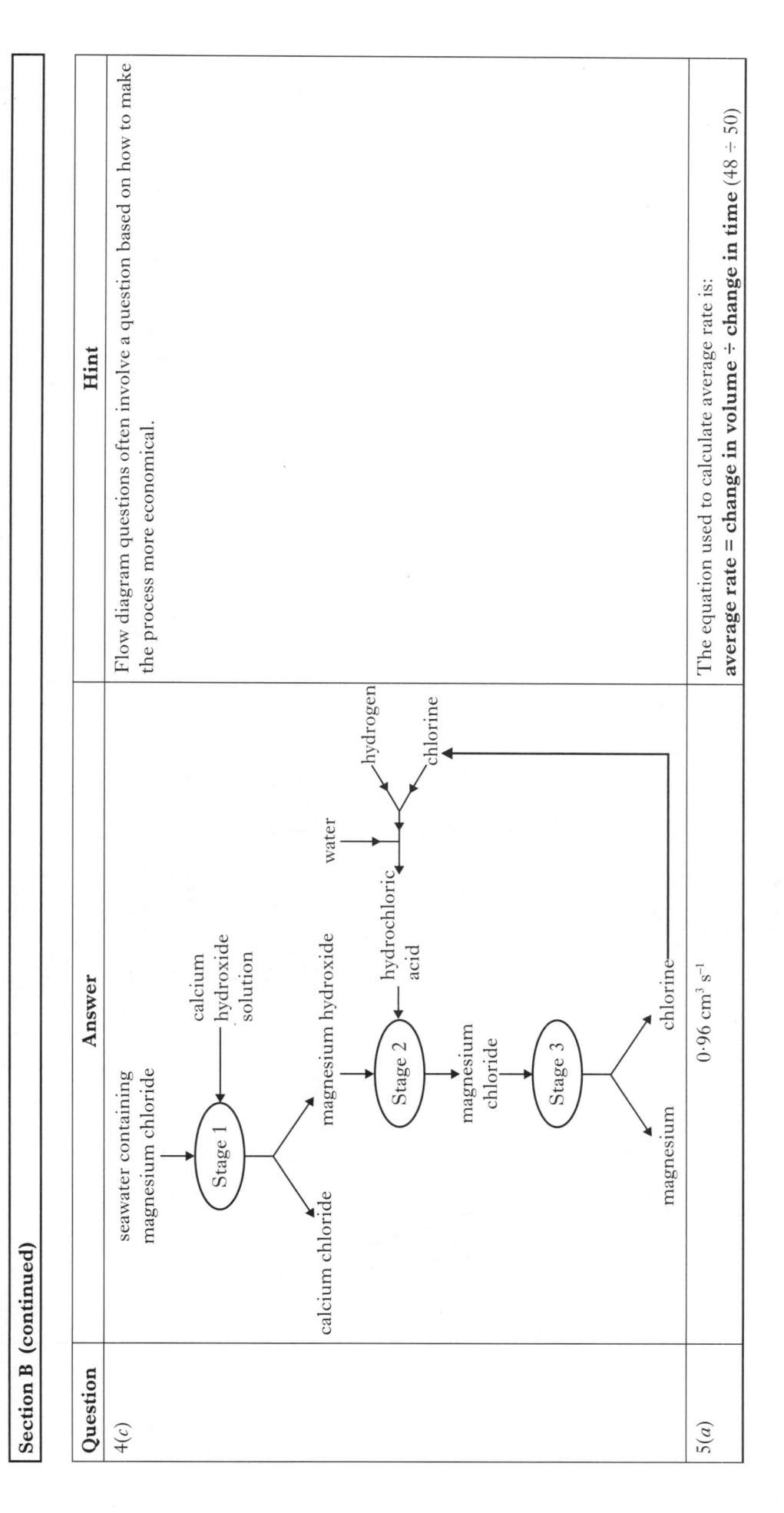

Question	Answer	Hint
4(c)	seawater containing magnesium chloride → Stage 1 (with calcium hydroxide solution added) → magnesium hydroxide → Stage 2 (with hydrochloric acid added; water and hydrogen produced, chlorine fed in) → magnesium chloride → Stage 3 → chlorine (recycled back to Stage 2) and magnesium. Stage 1 also produces calcium chloride.	Flow diagram questions often involve a question based on how to make the process more economical.
5(a)	0·96 cm³ s⁻¹	The equation used to calculate average rate is: **average rate = change in volume ÷ change in time** (48 ÷ 50)

Section B (continued)

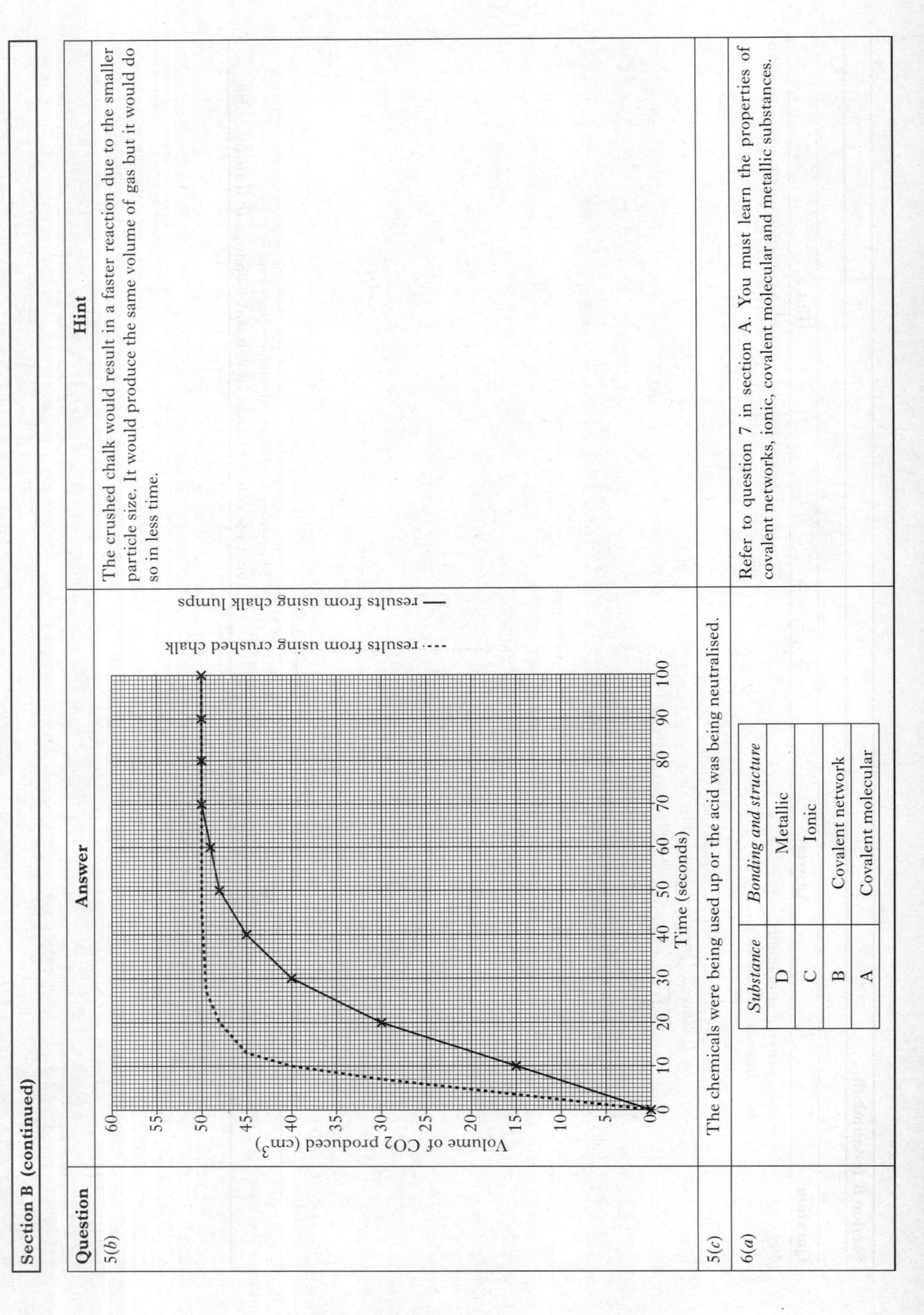

Question	Answer	Hint
5(b)	(Graph: Volume of CO_2 produced (cm^3) vs Time (seconds). Two curves plotted — dotted line: results from using crushed chalk; solid line with × markers: results from using chalk lumps. Both level off around 50 cm^3, with crushed chalk reaching the plateau much faster.)	The crushed chalk would result in a faster reaction due to the smaller particle size. It would produce the same volume of gas but it would do so in less time.
5(c)	The chemicals were being used up or the acid was being neutralised.	
6(a)		Refer to question 7 in section A. You must learn the properties of covalent networks, ionic, covalent molecular and metallic substances.

Substance	Bonding and structure
D	Metallic
C	Ionic
B	Covalent network
A	Covalent molecular

Practice Papers for SQA Exams: Intermediate 2 Chemistry Answers to Exam 2

Section B (continued)

Question	Answer	Hint
6(b)	A polar covalent bond arises when there is unequal sharing of electrons between the elements in the molecule. This results in an unequal sharing of the electrons in the bond, creating a dipole.	This may seem like a long answer for 1 mark but always give as much information as you can in an answer to ensure that you get the mark. It also helps to impress the examiner!
6(c)	The dipoles in water molecules allow weak forces of attraction to form between the molecules, so increasing the boiling point.	Water has unusual properties because of the weak forces of attraction that form between the molecules.
7(a)	<table><tr><th>Hydrocarbon</th><th>Molecular formula</th><th>Observations on adding bromine solution</th><th>Saturated or unsaturated?</th></tr><tr><td>A</td><td>C_6H_{14}</td><td>Remains orange</td><td>Saturated</td></tr><tr><td>B</td><td>C_6H_{12}</td><td>**Orange to colourless**</td><td>Unsaturated</td></tr><tr><td>C</td><td>C_6H_{12}</td><td>**Remains orange**</td><td>Saturated</td></tr><tr><td>D</td><td>C_6H_{10}</td><td>Orange to colourless</td><td>Unsaturated</td></tr></table>	This question is based on the PPA 'Testing for Unsaturation'.
7(b)	Any of the following: (structural formulae of C_6H_{12} isomers shown)	Always check that each carbon atom has four bonds when drawing full structural formulae.

Practice Papers for SQA Exams: Intermediate 2 Chemistry Answers to Exam 2

Section B (continued)

Question	Answer	Hint
7(c)	Isomers	Isomers have the same molecular formula but different structural formulae.
7(d)	Wear gloves/wear safety goggles/no naked flames	Bromine solution is also corrosive and spillages or splashes on the skin should be washed with sodium thiosulphate solution.
8(a)	H-C(=O)-O-CH(H)-C(H)(H)-H (structural formula shown)	Always check that each carbon atom has formed four bonds only when drawing full structural formulae.
8(b)	Ethanol	The first part of the ester name comes from the alcohol that was used to produce it.
8(c)	Condensation reaction	Esters are produced by a condensation reaction between an alkanol and an alkanoic acid.
9(a)	To keep constant positive and negative electrodes, or so that only one product is produced at each electrode.	This question is based on the PPA 'Electrolysis'.
9(b)	$2Cl^- + Cu^{2+} \rightarrow Cl_2 + Cu$	The electrons cancel each other out and should not be included in the redox equation.
9(c)	Positive electrode	Opposites attract! The negatively charged chloride ion would be attracted to the positive electrode.
10(a)	Oxygen and water	Oxygen and water are required for any metal to corrode.
10(b)	Oxidation	The iron atoms lose electrons to form iron ions during corrosion. **OIL RIG**. This can be show as an ion-electron equation: $Fe \rightarrow Fe_2^+ + 2e^-$.
10(c)	Zinc	Galvanising is the coating of zinc onto iron or steel. An easy way to remember this is to spell it the American way – Galvani**Z**ing!
10(d)	Test tube C	Sacrificial protection involves attaching a metal higher than iron in the electrochemical series. The metal will provide the iron with electrons, so reventing it from corroding. In test tube B the rate of corrosion would be very high because the iron is attached to a less reactive metal which will take electrons from the iron.
11(a)	To provide oxygen for the reaction.	This question is from the PPA 'Reaction of Metals with Oxygen'.

Practice Papers for SQA Exams: Intermediate 2 Chemistry Answers to Exam 2

Section B (continued)

Question	Answer	Hint
11(b)	Magnesium → zinc → copper	This should be straightforward but pay attention to the question and list the metals from the most to the least reactive.
11(c)	Magnesium	Reactive metals are extracted from their ore by electrolysis. This list shows how the metals are extracted from their ores. • K, Na, Li, Ca, Mg and Al – electrolysis of molten ore • Zn, Fe, Sn, Pb and Cu – heat with carbon or carbon monoxide • Hg, Ag, Au and Pt – heat alone
12	303 g	Top tip for questions involving $n = C \times V$: The volume of the solution is already in **litres** so there is no need to divide it by 1000. Step 1 Calculate the number of moles of potassium nitrate required using $n = C \times V$ ($2 \times 1 \cdot 5 = 3$ moles) (1 mark) Step 2 Work out the formula mass (FM) of potassium nitrate using its formula. $KNO_3 = 1 \times K(39) + 1 \times N(14) + 3 \times O(16)$ $= 39 + 14 + 48 = 101$ g Step 3 Calculate the mass of NaOH required using mass = moles × FM ($3 \times 101 = 303$ g) (1 mark)
13(a)	Aluminium oxide or silicate catalyst	Aluminium oxide is the more commonly used catalyst.
13(b)	The catalyst allows the reaction to be performed at a lower temperature.	In industry, if energy can be saved then profits increase.
13(c)	$C_{10}H_{22} \rightarrow C_6H_{14} + \mathbf{C_4H_8}$	This should be an easy one. The number of carbon and hydrogen atoms must be equal on each side of the equation.
13(d)	The molecule contains a carbon-to-carbon double bond.	Alkenes are unsaturated.
13(e)	Bromine water	Bromine is decolourised by unsaturated hydrocarbons. An addition reaction occurs between the bromine and the unsaturated hydrocarbon.
14(a)	Man-made	All plastics are synthetic.
14(b)	Thermoplastic	Thermoplastics soften on heating and can be reshaped. Thermosetting plastics do not soften on heating.

EXAM 3 — WORKED ANSWERS

SECTION A

Question	Answer	Hint
1	C	An easy one to get you started. Elements in the same group have similar chemical properties.
2	D	If the name of a compound ends in –ate or –ite then the compound also contains oxygen.
3	A	Experiment 2 produces half the amount of carbon dioxide so 0·5 g of chalk would have been used. The graph is less steep which means that it is a slower reaction than experiment 1 and so lumps will have been used in place of powder.
4	A	This is very similar to question 1. Elements in the same group all have the same number of outer electrons. This is what gives them similar properties.
5	A	It is important to know what a heterogeneous catalyst is and how it works. You don't need to know how a homogeneous catalyst works.
6	B	This question is asking you what an isotope is but in a more difficult way. Isotopes have the same atomic number but different mass numbers. The difference in mass is due to the atoms having a different number of neutrons.
7	D	A simple data book question.
8	B	You should be able to give examples of covalent networks such as diamond, graphite, and silicon dioxide. All other covalent compounds that you will deal with are covalent molecular compounds.
9	B	In solids, mobile electrons are required to allow conduction of electricity. In solutions, mobile ions are required for conduction of electricity to take place.
10	A	Don't let this question catch you out. The number of moles of oxygen or methane present has no effect on the balancing of the equation. Just balance the equation as normal. In this case some of the methane will remain unreacted.
11	D	It is important to learn all the various types of reactions and to be able to identify them.
12	C	Nitrogen dioxide is produced by the spark plugs in a petrol engine.
13	D	Isomers have the same molecular formula but different structural formulae. This means that they have the same numbers of each element in them but organised in a different way. Molecule D has more hydrogen atoms and is therefore not an isomer.
14	B	When naming esters it is important to remember that the carbon chain that has the =O attached came from the carboxylic acid. When naming esters remember: **alcohol to front, acid to back!**
15	D	Not another flow diagram! I hoped you paid attention to question 11. It is important to learn all the various types of reactions because many of them will be covered in the exam.
16	A	Have you learned all the various types of reaction yet?
17	A	Ethanol is produced from sugar by fermentation. The sugar used is obtained by growing sugar cane.

Page 90

Practice Papers for SQA Exams: Intermediate 2 Chemistry Answers to Exam 3

SECTION A (continued)

Question	Answer	Hint
18	C	Learn the formulae of all the carbohydrates. Monosaccharide – glucose and fructose – $C_6H_{12}O_6$ Disaccharide – sucrose and maltose – $C_{12}H_{22}O_{11}$ Polysaccharide – starch – $(C_6H_{10}O_5)_n$
19	C	When proteins are hydrolysed the peptide link breaks to form amino acids.
20	B	Esters are produced by reacting carboxylic acids with alcohols.
21	A	The ion bridge and electrolytes complete the circuit.
22	D	The copper would take electrons from the iron and increase the rate of corrosion. The iron must be attached to a metal above it in the reactivity series to be protected from corrosion.
23	D	**OIL RIG**. Oxidation is loss, so the Fe^{2+} ion must lose an electron to form Fe^{3+} ion.
24	C	Hydroxide ions cause ferroxyl indicator to turn pink and Fe^{2+} ions turn it blue.
25	D	$C = n \div V$ ($0.3 \div 0.1 = 3$ mol l^{-1}). Remember the volume must be in litres.
26	A	Hydrochloric acid is a strong acid and will therefore have a low pH.
27	D	Only carbonates react with acids to produce carbon dioxide gas. Because copper(II) carbonate is insoluble then the answer must be potassium carbonate.
28	B	This should be straightforward. Aluminium is a fairly reactive metal and copper, mercury and gold are all unreactive metals.
29	B	In all precipitation reactions, pay close attention to the state symbols. A precipitate is an insoluble **solid**.
30	C	Spectator ions are present in a reaction but are unchanged by it and so they appear on both sides of the equation completely unchanged.

Page 91

SECTION B

Question	Answer	Hint
1(a)	Glycerol	Hydrolysis of a fat or oil produces glycerol. Glycerol has the systematic name propane-1,2,3-triol.
1(b)	Fats	You should be able to explain why fats have a higher melting point than oils. Fat molecules can pack closer together, allowing the formation of intermolecular bonds. Look up a diagrammatic representation of fats and oils as this makes it very clear why the boiling points are so different.
1(c)	Esters	Fats and oils all have the COO functional group.
1(d)	Contains single carbon-to-carbon bonds	Oils contain more carbon to carbons double bonds and therefore have a lower melting point.
2(a)	X = 22 s Y = 0·0303 s^{-1}	To calculate X manipulate the equation $rate = 1 \div time$ to make it $time = 1 \div rate$ $(1 \div 0·0454 = 22)$. To calculate Y, $rate = 1 \div time$ $(1 \div 33 = 0·0303)$.
2(b)	At the end-point the solution would turn from colourless to blue/black.	It is essential to learn all the PPAs in detail. The PPA covered here is from Unit 1 – 'Effect of Concentration on Reaction Rate'
2(c)	Correct scale and axis labelled correctly (1 mark) Points plotted correctly (1 mark)	To gain all the marks in graph questions make sure you do the following: 1. Make sure the graph is as big as the graph paper allows. 2. Always draw a line of best fit using a pencil. 3. Label both axes correctly and clearly including the units. 4. Make sure the points are correctly plotted.

Practice Papers for SQA Exams: Intermediate 2 Chemistry Answers to Exam 3

SECTION B (continued)

Question	Answer	Hint
2(d)	To ensure that the concentration of all the other reactants remains constant.	This question should be straightforward if you have studied and learned all your PPA reports.
3(a)	Displacement	Displacement reactions involve both oxidation and reduction reactions.
3(b)	The Mg would react with the oxygen.	Reactions are often carried out in atmospheres of inert (unreactive) gases such as the noble gases and nitrogen. This avoids unwanted reactions.
3(c)	Covalent bonding (molecular)	The low melting point of 64·8°C suggests that the bonding is covalent.
4(a)	Methanoic acid dissociates only partially in water. Hydrochloric acid dissociates completely in water. (1 mark) This results in a high pH for methanoic acid as it has a lower concentration of H$^+$ ions which also results in lower conductivity. (1 mark)	This question tests your knowledge of strong and weak acids.
4(b)	HCl → H$^+$ + Cl$^-$	The single arrow indicates that it dissociates completely.
5(a)	Blue to brick red/orange	The PPA covered here is from Unit 2 – 'Hydrolysis of Starch'.
5(b)	To neutralise the acid catalyst.	This question should be straightforward.
5(c)	The control is to ensure that the enzyme and acid were responsible for the hydrolysis reaction.	Controls are used in most experiments of this type.
6(a)	Full structural formula of propan-1-ol (H–C(H)(H)–C(H)(H)–C(H)(H)–O–H)	When drawing full structural formulae, always ensure that each carbon atom has formed four bonds.
6(b)	Propan-1-ol	Isomer questions are always easier if you draw the structure on a spare piece of paper.
6(c)	0·01 moles	Top tip for questions involving moles = mass ÷ formula mass: Be careful when calculating the formula mass as this is where most mistakes are made. Step 1 Work out the formula mass (FM) of propan-2-ol using its molecular formula. C$_3$H$_7$OH = 3 × C(12) + 7 × H(1) + 1 × O(16) + 1 × H(1) = 36 + 7 + 16 + 1 = 60 g (1 mark) Step 2 Calculate the number of moles of propan-2-ol using moles = mass ÷ formula mass (0·6 ÷ 60 = 0·01 moles) (1 mark)

Page 93

SECTION B (continued)

Question	Answer	Hint
7(a)	voltmeter, V, zinc, electrolyte sodium chloride, iron (labelled diagram)	The PPA covered here is from Unit 3 – Factors Affecting Voltage. Markers assess these questions by asking themselves 'Will the experiment work as drawn?' Ensure that the diagram is clearly labelled and not too small.
7(b)	Al → Zn 0·6 to 0·7 V	Electrons flow from the more reactive to the less reactive metal. Use your knowledge of the reactivity series and your data booklet to estimate the voltage that would be produced.
7(c)	Any two from: Temperature Concentration of electrolyte Volume of electrolyte Distance between electrodes	These factors should have been included in your write-up for the PPA.
8(a)	Branched hydrocarbons have higher octane numbers.	The answer is in the table. Compare hexane with 2-methylpentane.
8(b)	Zero (±2)	This is a very difficult question. The difference between hexane and its isomer 2-methylpentane is 46. So you can expect the difference between heptane and its isomer to be roughly the same.
8(c)	Isomers	Isomers have the same molecular formula but different structural formulae.
9	1 mol l^{-1}	There are several ways to do this calculation. Here is the $P \times V \times C_{(acid)} = P \times V \times C_{(alkali)}$ method. Power = number of H$^+$ or OH$^-$ ions. Volume in litres. Concentration in mol l^{-1}. $P \times V \times C_{(acid)} = P \times V \times C_{(alkali)}$ $1 \times 0·01 \times C = 1 \times 0·02 \times 0·5$ $0·01 \times C = 0·01$ $C = 0·01 \div 0·01$ $C = 1$ mol l^{-1} This question can also be answered using the balanced equation and moles = concentration × volume.

SECTION B (continued)

Question	Answer	Hint
10(a)	[Diagram showing: bunsen burner, water condensing, ice and water, limewater turns cloudy, to suction pump]	Markers assess these questions by asking themselves 'Will the experiment work as drawn?' Ensure that the delivery tube on the left is in the limewater and the delivery tube on the right is above the limewater.
10(b)	To condense any water vapour that is produced.	Sometimes cobalt paper is placed in the tube to detect any water produced.
10(c)	Soot is produced due to incomplete combustion.	When soot is produced or the flame is yellow it is a sure sign of incomplete combustion due to a poor oxygen supply.
11(a)	Galvanising	Galvanising also has a different spelling – galvaniZing: this can make it easier to remember.
11(b)	Oxygen and water	An easy one for a change!
11(c)	Steel is an alloy made mostly of iron. If the zinc coating is scratched then the zinc will provide sacrificial protection (1 mark) because it is more reactive than iron. Tin however is less reactive than iron and would therefore increase the rate of corrosion because it would take electrons from the iron. (1 mark)	Give as much detail as you can in questions like this to ensure you get the marks. The answer shown perhaps gives too much information but it is better to give more detail rather than not enough.
12(a)	All metals have electrons that are free to move (i.e. delocalised).	In solids, mobile electrons are required to allow conduction of electricity. In solutions, mobile ions are required for conduction of electricity to take place.

SECTION B (continued)

Question	Answer	Hint
12(b)	$Cu + Cl_2 \rightarrow CuCl_2$	The equation will be balanced if you remembered that chlorine is diatomic and then worked out the correct formula of copper(II) chloride.
12(c)	Each chlorine atoms gains an electron from the copper atom so that the chlorine ions formed have the electron arrangement 2, 8, 8.	A stable electron arrangement is only achieved when an element has a stable outer energy level like that of a noble gas.
12(d)	$Cu^{2+} + 2e^- \rightarrow Cu$	The positive copper ions are attracted to the negative electrode. The charge on the copper ions is indicated in the compound name: copper(II) chloride. The number in brackets indicates that copper has a valency or charge of 2.
13(a)	Addition polymerisation	The clue is in the structure of styrene. The carbon-to-carbon double bond suggests that the type of polymerisation that will take place is addition.
13(b)	*[structural diagram of polystyrene section]*	To show that only a section of the polymer chain has been drawn, the end bonds must be left open.
13(c)	Softens and can be reshaped on heating.	Thermo**setting** plastics are **set**. They will not soften on heating.
14(a)	Carbon dioxide and nitrogen	Catalytic converters convert harmful gases into less harmful gases.
14(b)	Incomplete combustion	This question is similar to question 10(c).
14(c)	Diesel engines do not have spark plugs.	Nitrogen dioxide is produced by sparking air. This happens naturally in lightning storms but also happens when the air/petrol mixture is sparked in a petrol engine. In diesel engines there are no spark plugs and therefore no NO_2 is produced.
14(d)	A catalyst that is in a different state to the reactants.	An easy one to finish off!